ALBERT EINSTEIN

The Jewish Man Behind the Theory

Publication of this book was made possible by a gift from

DAVID FRANKEL

in memory of his beloved wife,

ANN FRANKEL,

whose devotion to her family knew no bounds

ALBERT EINSTEIN

The Jewish Man Behind the Theory

DEVRA NEWBERGER SPEREGEN

2006 • 5766
THE JEWISH PUBLICATION SOCIETY
Philadelphia

The Jewish Publication Society
2100 Arch Street, 2nd floor
Philadelphia, PA 19103
www.jewishpub.org

Design and Composition by Book Design Studio II

Manufactured in the United States of America

06 07 08 09 10   10 9 8 7 6 5 4 3 2 1

Library of Congress Cataloging-in-Publication Data

Speregen, Devra Newberger.
 Albert Einstein : the Jewish man behind the theory / by Devra Newberger Speregen.-
- 1st ed.
   p. cm.
 Includes bibliographical references and index.
 ISBN 0-8276-0824-1 (alk. paper)
 1. Einstein, Albert, 1879-1955. 2. Physicists--United States--Biography. 3. Physicists--Germany--Biography. 4. Jewish scientists--United States--Biography. 5. Jewish scientists--Germany--Biography. 6. Jews--Israel--Identity. I. Title.
 QC16.E5S648 2006
 530.092--dc22

2005029960

CONTENTS

This book is dedicated to all young Jewish thinkers

… and to mine personally:

Jordy Speregen, Halle Speregen,

Elad Newberger, and Samson Newberger.

ACKNOWLEDGMENTS

I am grateful to many for the opportunity to write this biography: To Dr. Ellen Frankel, Carol Hupping, and Janet Liss at The Jewish Publication Society, and to my husband, Adam. And I'm especially grateful to my parents, Shirley and Joel Newberger, for their expertise and guidance in all things editorial and physics-related. (Everything is relative!)

Devra Newberger Speregen

INTRODUCTION

*I believe in intuitions and inspirations...I sometimes feel that I am right.
I do not know that I am.*

Albert Einstein, 1929

*The important thing is not to stop questioning. Curiosity has its own
reason for existing. One cannot help but be in awe when one contem-
plates the mysteries of eternity, of life, of the marvelous structure of
reality. It is enough if one tries to comprehend only a little of this
mystery every day.*

Albert Einstein, 1955

Albert Einstein was a modest man whose face became the most
recognizable face in the world. Both adored and despised by mil-
lions, this complex and controversial scientist was one of the greatest thinkers of all time. The son of a man who could never succeed
in the electronics business, he grew to become a renowned physicist who radically transformed our understanding of the universe.

From a seemingly ordinary family background, he went on to lead a most extraordinary life. Today it is hard to imagine what our world would be like if there had never been an Albert Einstein.

From his earliest years, Einstein showed his inquisitive nature and limitless imagination. He passionately asked questions about the mysteries of the universe: "Why is the sky blue? Where does the universe end? Why does the needle on a compass always point north?" And from all this thinking and questioning, answers and amazing discoveries would eventually emerge.

In 1905, when Einstein was only 26, he published a series of scientific papers. In one of them, he developed an equation $E=mc^2$—the equation that would forever change the thinking of the entire scientific world. He used this formula to develop his special theory of relativity that helped physicists unlock such mysteries as energy and matter, gravity and magnetism, motion, time, and space. With this equation, Einstein helped scientists to understand how light can act as both particles and waves, how atoms can emit radiation, and how speed and gravity affect time. His findings have been an important part of making many of our common devices work today. Laser surgery, photocopiers, digital cameras, DVDs, and solar-powered devices—none would have been possible without the contributions of Albert Einstein. Discoveries in photoelectronics and light waves, which eventually would lead to more discoveries in satellites and computers, owe their existence to the theoretical framework he created.

In 2005, Einstein's special theory of relativity and the journal in which he presented his famous $E=mc^2$ equation celebrated their 100th anniversary. Around the world, memorabilia such as bumper stickers, mouse pads, videos, license plates, and t-shirts that carry his famous formula, were circulated in honor of the annus mirabilis (the miracle year) of the equation. One hundred years later, technologists are still finding new ways to create new inventions using all that's been learned from Einstein's theories.

For most of mankind, the triumph of Albert Einstein is certainly an outstanding legacy. But for Jews, his accomplishments hold exceptional meaning. Jewish children around the world can claim an inheritance of imagination and curiosity from the greatest physicist of all time. More importantly, Jewish people everywhere owe a debt to Albert Einstein for his help in the creation of Israel.

Even though Einstein did not embrace a particular philosophy or religion in his scientific findings, he has, for 100 years, inspired Jews. Not only was Einstein successful in the world of physics, but his tireless fundraising efforts for the Zionist cause and his willingness to travel all over the world to spread the ideals of Zionism gave Jews everywhere the courage and strength to believe in the reality of a Jewish homeland. And although he never settled in Israel, he lived long enough to witness the creation of the State and was proud to have been instrumental in making it happen.

Albert Einstein was often asked how he became a genius. Was it a trait inherited from his father, an easygoing, German-born man who failed in one business after another, or from his mother, who was often described by Einstein as a noble, quiet woman with a passion for music? Einstein believed that his intellectual ability stemmed, in part, from his Jewish heritage. Despite his upbringing in a non-observant Jewish home, as a child he still managed to embrace his Jewish roots. Later, as an adult, he consistently surrounded himself with great Jewish thinkers and artists—Sigmund Freud, Madame Curie, and Marc Chagall, to name a few of his great friends—and he devoted his studies to the writings and philosophies of great Jews.

Was Einstein correct that it was in his Jewish genes to become a genius? Or did the life and times in which he lived shape his remarkable intelligence? Most likely, genius comes from a combination of both these things.

As we explore his incredible life and work, we will come to understand the depth of Einstein's contributions to both science and the Zionist cause. Einstein lived and worked most of his life in Germany—a country that hated him for being a Jew and a genius during the era of the worst anti-Semitism the Jewish people have ever encountered. We will learn how his ability to succeed in this environment, despite some extraordinary difficulties, makes him one of the world's most important Jewish heroes.

1

The Einsteins

Strange is our situation here on Earth. Each of us comes for a short visit, not knowing why, yet sometimes seeming to divine a purpose.

Albert Einstein, 1932

Tracing Albert Einstein's roots, nothing extraordinary stands out that would indicate the birth of this genius in Prussia on March 14, 1879.

In 1577, Jews had begun to settle in Prussia (then the northern region of Germany) and formed respectable communities where they prospered. During the late 1800s, Germany grew strong and Prussia became the most powerful region of Germany, known best for its military strength. Albert Einstein's family (both his father's and mother's families) came from this quiet region of Germany, where the people there were mainly shopkeepers, shoemakers, craftsmen, and traders.

Albert's father, Hermann Einstein, came from Buchau, a small community in Wurttemberg (in Prussia). Despite, the atrocities committed against Jews during World War

II in the 1930s and 1940s, Jews continued to live in Buchau until 1968 when the last Jew in Buchau was reported to have died. This last Jew, in fact, was a distant relative of Albert Einstein's: Siegbert Einstein.

On his paternal side, Albert Einstein's family can be traced back to Buchau in the late 1700s, when his great-grandfather Ruppert Einstein was born. He lived in Buchau and married Rebekka Obernauer. Their son, Abraham Einstein (Albert's grandfather), was born in 1808. Abraham (who died before Albert was born) was said to have been an intelligent, respected man. He, too, lived in Buchau and later married Helene (Hindel) Moos. Their son, Hermann Einstein (Albert's father), was born in Buchau on August 30, 1847.

In 1866, when Hermann Einstein was nineteen, his family moved north to Ulm, an old town on the Danube River, nestled in the foothills of the Swabian Alps. Hermann worked there at a feather-bedding firm called Israel and Levi. Ulm was a small town where Jews retained their own separate Jewish identity yet lived at ease among the rest of the German community. In 1876, Hermann met and married Pauline Koch (Albert's mother), a woman eleven years younger than he.

The Koch family had been part of the Jewish community in Ulm for more than a century. Pauline was the daughter of Julius Derzbacher and Jette Bernheim (they later took the family name Koch). Julius, an energetic man with an interest in art, was a baker by trade. He eventually worked as a grain merchant and made a considerable fortune in the corn trade. He became so successful in the corn trade that he sold corn exclusively to the Royal family in Wurttemberg and was named "Royal Wurttemberg Purveyor to the Court."

Einstein's father, Hermann Einstein. (Hebrew University of Jerusalem Albert Einstein Archives—Courtesy of AIP Emilio Segre Visual Archives.)

Jette, Albert's maternal grandmother, was a quiet, good-natured woman with a sense of humor. For many years, Julius and Jette lived in a house with Julius' brother and his family. Sharing a house was rare in Germany, but it worked out well for the two families and Pauline grew up in a happy home filled with siblings and cousins.

Hermann Einstein, Albert's father, was a friendly man, who may have not had a head for business, but was nonetheless intelligent and hard-working. He enjoyed taking his family on weekly hikes into the beautiful countryside around Munich to visit lakes and mountains and would often stop for lunch at a quaint Bavarian tavern to feast on beer and sausages. Later in life, Albert Einstein fondly recalled those Sunday excursions with his family, remembering how his parents would playfully argue about where they should go and which routes they should take to get there.

Hermann showed a knack for mathematics early on and had hoped to pursue his studies in this field, but because his father was struggling to make ends meet, this was not possible. Instead, Hermann was obligated to help out his family financially. So he worked in Ulm as a merchant along with a close cousin.

Einstein's mother Pauline was a warm and caring woman, and the parent many regard as Albert's "creative inspiration." She introduced Albert to culture, music, and art. Pauline herself was a musician, a talented pianist and singer, as well as an avid reader who especially loved German literature.

In 1877, with money borrowed from Pauline's parents, Hermann set up a small electrical and engineering company a few yards away from their apartment in Ulm, deciding that would become his business. Two years

Einstein's mother, Pauline Koch Einstein. (Hebrew University of Jerusalem Albert Einstein Archives—Courtesy of AIP Emilio Segre Visual Archives.)

later Albert was born, and one year after that, sadly, the business collapsed. This wouldn't be the last time Hermann's family business failed; but to his credit, his good nature and high hopes never stopped him from trying. Hermann's family and that of and his younger brother, Jakob, moved again—this time to Munich, Germany—and started another business. This time they opened a small plumbing and electronics business called Einstein & Cie ("Company").

The move to Munich brought the Einstein family from a small, rural environment to the bustling capital of Bavaria to live among more than a quarter of a million people. Mostly Catholic, the city of Munich was very different from Ulm, filled with art galleries, breweries, and cathedrals, and with the constant sounds of church bells ringing in the air.

The Einsteins first lived in a small rented house in Munich, but after five years their family business became profitable and they were able to afford a larger home in the suburbs, a short distance away from the factory where Hermann manufactured the electrical equipment for his business. His brother Jakob had more technical knowledge, so Jakob worked on designing the equipment.

One year after the move to Munich, on November 18, 1881, Pauline gave birth to a baby girl to whom she and Hermann gave the name of Maria, but called her Maja. Of course, like any brother and sister, Albert and Maja had their share of sibling rivalry—there was even a period of a few years where the two didn't speak to one another. In spite of that, however, Albert and Maja soon became the best of friends. He eventually grew very close to his sister, a closeness that lasted throughout their lives.

Many Jews who lived in rural towns and suburban communities during the late 1800s were often more observant than those who lived in the cities. Munich, for example, was predominantly Catholic and the Jews who lived and worked there had mainly assimilated into Catholic life. Many Jews didn't belong to the local synagogue, didn't keep kosher, and did not follow the customs or traditions that are part of the Jewish faith.

The Einsteins were no different. They, too, soon assimilated into Munich's Catholic culture, even to the point where they sometimes celebrated Easter and Christmas. The Einsteins did adopt a few Jewish customs, but for the most part, they lived comfortably in Munich and did not participate in any formal religion. Albert was enrolled in Catholic schools, mostly for convenience, but also because his father didn't feel strong ties to Judaism. Albert would grow to challenge his parent's beliefs—even embracing Judaism on his own for a short time. Albert remained an "outsider" to his faith during childhood—a pattern that repeated itself throughout his young life. Later, Albert became a more philosophical thinker who felt more connected to God and Judaism and had a clearer understanding of their relation to nature and spirituality.

2

A Child Genius?

The pursuit of knowledge for its own sake, an almost fanatical love of justice, and the desire for personal independence—these are the features of the Jewish tradition which make me thank my lucky stars that I belong to it.

Albert Einstein, 1934

What was Albert like as a child? You might assume that he was an exceptionally smart boy who always received excellent grades at school and advanced quickly. After all, he grew up to be a genius, right? In fact, the opposite was really true. He was so slow to begin to speak as a child and so quiet that his parents often worried there was something wrong with him! He didn't really speak properly until he was nine years old, and even then he would take so long to answer a question, that his parents and teachers feared that he might never amount to anything. Once, when his father asked Albert's school headmaster what profession his son was best suited for, the headmaster replied, "It doesn't matter. He'll never make a success of anything."

Albert himself once remarked that his slow development and backwardness as a child actually helped him in the development of his scientific theories later as an adult. "The normal adult never thinks about space and time." he said. "These are thoughts he has thought about when he was a child. But since my intellectual development was retarded ...I began to wonder about space and time only when I had already grown up. Naturally, I could go deeper into the problem than a child with normal abilities."

In fact, from the moment Albert was born, his parents knew there was something just different about him. At birth, his mother was shocked at the sight of the back of his head, which was extremely large and angular. She feared she'd given birth to a sick, deformed child. But as the doctor assured her, after a few weeks the shape of baby Albert's skull became normal. Albert was also a fat baby. When his grandmother, Jette, first saw him, she threw up her hands in surprise and said over and over again: "Much too fat! Much too fat!" But as babies often do, Albert changed a lot during the first year of his life, and his head and body finally developed in proportion to his frame.

When Albert was two and his baby sister, Maja, was born, young Albert was sure she was a toy. He hadn't said a word up until this point, but after careful inspection of the newborn, he asked his parents, "Where are its wheels?" He didn't take much interest in his sister then, or even a few years later. Albert was a timid, awkward boy, and when Maja and other children would play outside together, he would often sit off to the side and occupy himself with quieter things, like puzzles or reading. Even the children's governess called slow-

A young Albert Einstein, ca. 1891.
(Hebrew University of Jerusalem Albert Einstein Archives—
Courtesy of AIP Emilio Segre Visual Archives.)

speaking Albert, "pater langweil," which means "father bore" in English.

In a written account of her brother's childhood, Maja remembered her older brother as a shy, quiet, thoughtful boy with some unusual habits. She wrote that until age seven, Albert would repeat every word or sentence he heard softly to himself, while moving his lips. She also remembered that her brother would often throw temper tantrums and had a violent nature as a young boy. She described how his face would turn yellow and the tip of his nose would grow white when he became very angry. On one occasion, when he was six years old, he threw a chair at a music teacher. On another occasion, he threw a heavy bowling ball at his sister's head! Luckily, his violent temper didn't last long and completely disappeared during his early school years. Much later, Maja wrote that "one needed an especially thick skull to be the sister of a genius!"

At age five, Albert began violin lessons, which he didn't enjoy at the time, but learned to love playing later on in life. In fact, he grew so passionate about the violin that in addition to becoming an exceptional scientist, he also became an accomplished musician. At age four, he was very self-sufficient. Maja described how her parents often sent Albert for walks alone through the busy streets of the city. They would show him the way to some place once and then the next time he was left to find his way alone. Little Albert had become exceptionally self-reliant, able to cross busy intersections and follow directions without help from adults.

One legendary story from Albert's childhood occurred when he was almost five. Albert was at home, sick in bed (or, more probably, he was refusing to go to school), and his father presented him with a small compass. Little Albert was amazed by the compass—how the needle would always point north, no matter if it was turned around or held upside-down. To Albert, there was some-thing magical about the tiny instrument. It fascinated him and he wondered about the compass for months, always determined to find the reason for this phenomenon. Years later, he wrote about the compass, "I can still remember that this experience made a deep and lasting impres-sion on me. Something deeply hidden had to be behind things." When he grew older, Albert learned more about magnets. He learned that it was the earth's magnetic field that made the needle point north.

At age seven, Albert entered secondary school (called Volksschule). He had a very strict teacher who would whack his students with *tatzen* (knuckle raps) on the back of their hands to get them to learn their multiplication tables. Because Albert was still slow to speak and respond to questions, he fell victim to many *tatzen*. His teachers considered him dull-witted, even stupid.

At school, Albert was the only Jewish student. He was too young to realize that German society at that time was anti-Semitic (a term that means hatred toward Jews) and that many Germans blamed the Jewish people for the country's money problems. But Albert was old enough to feel hurt when the other children teased him and called him names. They also ridiculed him mercilessly for not participating in any school sports.

At home, schoolwork was held in the highest regard. The rule was that homework always had to be finished before playtime could begin. Both Albert and Maja followed these rules, but when homework was complete and Maja would rush outdoors to join other children, Albert remained inside. Among his favorite toys were puzzles and building sets. He loved to create structures using many different materials, but he particularly enjoyed building complicated structures with his "Anker" building set (a construction toy set like Lego). He also spent much of his playtime building houses made from playing cards. A patient and precise boy, Albert could build a card house fourteen stories high!

The same year that Albert entered grade school, he was required by German law to begin his religious instruction. Since Catholicism was the only religion taught in school, Albert's parents enlisted a distant relative to give him Jewish instruction at home. Albert became quite infatuated by the Torah and Jewish philosophy and a deep, religious feeling was awakened within him as he studied about God and the Bible. He asked many, many questions about God. Albert became deeply religious during this period as a result of his informal Jewish education.

Later in life, Albert was quoted as saying: "I want to know how God created this world.... I am not interested in this or that phenomenon, in the spectrum of this or that element. I want to know his thoughts ... the rest are details."

As his private Jewish instruction continued, Albert became quite confused as to why his family wasn't more observant. Trying on many occasions to get them to adopt certain Jewish customs and beliefs, it often fell upon him to observe these customs alone. When he was about eleven years old he decided to keep kosher—refusing to eat pork. Albert felt that this and other traditional religious requirements should be obeyed and not ridiculed. But Albert's father, like so many German Jews of the time, dismissed organized religion as "superstition."

At age nine, Albert attended the Luitpold Gymnasium (a German high school) where there was a huge emphasis placed on studying the classical languages—Latin and Greek. To Albert's dismay, math and science were of much less importance in the curriculum. In fact, at Albert's school, structured education in algebra and geometry didn't begin until age thirteen. So, just as he had begun to study Judaism independently, Albert took it upon himself to learn math and science. With textbooks given to him by his parents, Albert spent all of his free time working on mathematical problems and trying to solve them. For days he would sit alone, immersed in the search for solutions, and would not give up until he found them. During his first summer vacation from school, Albert worked himself through the complete school syllabus in science

Albert and his sister, Maja. When this picture was taken,
Albert was about 14 and Maja about 12.
(Courtesy of the Leo Baeck Institute, New York.)

for the year! With help from his Uncle Jakob, who had studied mathematics and engineering, Albert was able to solve complicated mathematical problems. His uncle was astonished by how quickly his nephew caught on to many complex math theories. Throughout his life, Albert always remembered his Uncle Jakob for being instrumental in teaching him algebra—not so much for the material he chose to teach, but for the manner in which he taught it.

Even though his parents were not committed to their religion, Albert was glad that they still observed a few Jewish customs. A popular custom among Jews of that time was to invite a poor Jewish student to a family's home for dinner on Thursday night. One such person was a medical school student named Max Talmud (he later changed his last name to "Talmey") with whom Albert developed a close relationship. The two would spend hours after dinner discussing philosophy and science, and despite their age differences, Max treated Albert as an equal and a friend. To Albert's delight, Max would bring him books every week—books on science that Albert would devour the first night he got them. In just a few short months, Albert completed an entire set of science books, cover to cover!

Throughout his early teen years, Albert's musical abilities began to develop further. He played Mozart and Beethoven sonatas on the violin accompanied by his mother on the piano and spent many evenings at the piano creating arpeggios (accompaniment patterns of music) and searching for new melodies. He combined his ardent belief in God with his passion for the music of Mozart and Beethoven and he wrote songs about God, which he sang out loud while walking to and from school.

Music was an important part of Albert's life as he grew up. His sister, Maja, recalled that some of her happiest childhood moments were spent listening to Albert and their mother play duets. Years later, Albert reflected on the impact music had on him as a child. "I got most joy in life out of my violin," he told a reporter. "I often think in music. I live my daydreams in music. I see my life in terms of music."

Music was also the perfect distraction for Albert, a way to forget about his distressing situation at school. Albert hated school. He had no friends and his teachers complained about him. The teachers grew angry when he couldn't answer questions quickly enough and they grew tired of hearing him complain that he was bored. Some reprimanded him for asking too many questions! Albert compared his teachers to drill sergeants and he hated the military atmosphere at school.

By age 14, Albert had already mastered higher mathematics, which was not even taught in his secondary school. Calculus, geometry—he'd learned them all by himself. His mathematical knowledge amazed everyone at school, but his teachers still complained because they were embarrassed at not being able to answer many of Albert's difficult questions.

Although he was beginning to emerge as a genius in math and science, Albert was a poor student of languages. He could never master the Greek or Latin in school and was unable to grasp the rudiments of the Hebrew language taught by special instructors at home. For this reason, Albert decided against having a traditional bar mitzvah when he turned thirteen. "I often read the Bible," Albert said later on in life, "but its original text has remained beyond my reach."

Unfortunately, because he lacked the gift of memorization, his grades suffered miserably. In his school the students were taught by "rote." (Learning by rote is the practice of repeating and memorizing facts.) Since this was Albert's weakest area, he became an outcast among his classmates and humiliated by his teachers. Albert's grades in school were often so low that Hermann and Pauline were sure he would never graduate.

Albert's sister, Maja, however, always had faith in her brother and she grew to love him dearly. Later in life, Maja remembered how Albert had battled constantly with his teachers at school. She specifically remembered Albert's Greek professor, Dr. Joseph Degenhart, who, after reading a particularly poor paper Albert had turned in, shouted in anger that nothing would ever become of him. "Your mere presence here undermines the class's respect for me," the teacher is remembered to have said. Many years later, in a short biography she wrote about her brother's early childhood, Maja joked that perhaps that Greek professor had been right. "In fact," she wrote, "Albert Einstein never did attain a professorship in Greek grammar."

3

Leaving Germany

The Jew who abandons his faith (in the formal sense of the word) is in a position similar to a snail that abandons its shell. He remains a Jew.

Albert Einstein, 1938

In 1884, the Einstein family business met with failure again. Unable to compete with the larger electrical and plumbing companies, Hermann was forced to close his shop and look for another way to provide for his family. He eventually decided to move his family from Germany to Italy to live there with relatives while he pursued a new business.

The problem was what to do with Albert who was just one year shy of completing his studies at school. If Albert moved to Italy, he would need to learn Italian in order to enroll in and finish high school. That didn't seem possible given his difficulty with languages. So another tough decision was made: Albert would be left in Munich to live with another family at a boarding house until he finished out the school year.

Albert had never been a good student, had never liked school, and his time spent at the gymnasium had been particularly unpleasant. High school had been just like his elementary and secondary schools. The teaching style of the German teachers was based on strict discipline with an emphasis on religion and obeying authority. Rules were strictly enforced, and those who questioned them were met with thrashings and harsh words. The atmosphere was brutal. The gymnasium was primarily a place where Germans prepared their children to become soldiers.

Albert continued to experience anti-Semitism in school. One day, his religion teacher brought a large nail to class and told the students that it was the nail with which the Jews had nailed Jesus to the cross. This incident ended up sparking a deeper hatred for Albert by his classmates, for he was the only Jewish student in class.

Albert was miserable in school and as soon as his family left for Italy, he was determined to find a way out of school—one that would enable him to move to Italy and join them. Italy, Albert imagined, was a paradise. He'd heard a great deal about the country from his cousins who lived in Genoa and had visited him in Munich. Soon he received letters from his parents and sister describing a land of sun, culture, and free, nature-loving people.

Alone in Munich, Albert grew more and more depressed, struggling through school and living at the boarding house. He hated life at the boarding house, primarily because he had no place to practice his violin. Quiet hours were observed there and that meant no music after school. Finally, the opportunity Albert had been waiting for presented itself. Albert's teacher scolded him one day and then threatened to expel him. Albert seized the chance to make a break from the school. He obtained a letter from the school physician that claimed he was suffering from nervous exhaustion and depression over being separated from his family. He presented the letter to the gymnasium directors, who were planning to expel him anyway. After he assured them that he would continue his studies in Italy and prepare himself for college entrance exams, they agreed to let him leave.

According to the German citizenship laws at the time, a male citizen could not leave the country until he has completed school at the age of sixteen. Every boy of that age was required to enter the military to prepare to become a soldier. This was even more reason for 16-year-old Albert to leave Germany. He'd never wanted to become a soldier. After watching a military parade at the age of five, he knew that he could never become a soldier. He hated the thought of war and the German soldiers frightened him. So Albert decided that it would be best to renounce his German citizenship so that he could leave Germany and move to Italy. Although this may have been a drastic step to take for a 16-year-old, Albert stood firm on his decision. He had decided to leave the bleakness of Munich for the warmth of sunny Italy.

Albert surprised his parents in Italy when he arrived unannounced in Milan with all his belongings. Even though his parents were happy to see their son, they were alarmed that he had dropped out of school and renounced his German citizenship. They worried what would become of him. How would he complete his education? How could he live and work in Italy, not knowing the language and or having any money of his own? But Albert wasn't worried. He diligently resumed his mathematical and scientific studies while he worked part time in the family factory. He was determined to complete his high school education and set his sights on attending college in Switzerland.

The freer, independent life in Italy really suited Albert. He traveled as much as possible, backpacking through the country, learning whatever he could about the Italian culture and way of life. Everything about the country appealed to him—especially how much of it differed from the bleak, military atmosphere in Germany. The people of Italy seemed happy and friendly, with a passion for music and art. Albert immediately felt at home and made up his mind never to return to Germany.

While Albert was enjoying his new life in Italy, his father's electrical engineering business was failing and it ultimately closed. Albert was forced to concern himself with his future. He needed money to help provide for his family. He needed a profession and a clearer direction in his life. With no real options, there was nothing left for Albert to do but to find a technical profession, perhaps become an engineer somewhere. His hope was to gain a technical (business) degree, work in Italy, and live a modest life on a small income. Unfortunately, he was too young to attend technical school—he had yet to graduate from high school!

With a letter that he had obtained from his math teacher back at the Luitpold Gymnasium, in which the teacher had praised Albert's math skills, Albert applied for admission to the Confederate Polytechnic Academy in Zurich, Switzerland. Since he had never graduated from high school in Munich, he was told that he would have to pass an entrance exam in order to enroll at the Academy. While Albert certainly had the math and science skills to pass this exam, he unfortunately didn't pass because of his poor language skills. He now needed to find another way to finish high school.

In 1895, Albert enrolled at the Kantonalschule (high school) in Aarau, Switzerland, about twenty miles from Zurich. He chose this school because the population in Aarau spoke mostly German (the town was on the Swiss-German border) and he wouldn't need to learn another language in order to enroll. The situation seemed perfect. He could complete his schooling at Kantonalschule, then apply for enrollment at the Academy once he had received his diploma. Albert felt some sense of relief now that he had a plan for the future.

Though excited, Albert was first apprehensive about going back to school, remembering his strict school days in Munich. He was pleasantly surprised, however, to find an entirely different spirit at Kantonalschule: It was a freer, more pleasant environment with different classrooms for each subject. The teachers were not strict—some were even friendly—and Albert felt immediately comfortable. He even made friends and began to enjoy living in Aarau almost as much as he'd enjoyed Italy.

Albert arranged to live with a teacher at the school, a professor named Jost Winteler, his wife, and their seven children. Amazingly, even with all those children, Albert still had his own bedroom at the Winteler home! Professor Winteler, a kind man, taught German and history at the school, and Albert learned a lot from him. He especially enjoyed becoming part of the professor's family, traveling with them, meeting new people, and visiting new places. Years later, he became even closer to the Winteler family when his sister, Maja, married one of their sons.

Living with the Wintelers was wonderful for Albert. The children treated him as one of the family, and the parents welcomed him with such affection that he soon called them by endearing Swiss nicknames for mother and father. Dinnertime was Albert's favorite time of the day when the professor engaged in discussions about history and classical literature, encouraging everyone at the table to participate.

On weekends, Albert accompanied Professor Winteler and some other students on hikes into the countryside to stalk rare birds or observe the flora and fauna. On occasion, the professor's daughter, Marie, would join them. Marie was 18 years old and was studying to become a teacher. Albert took an interest in Marie, and it wasn't long before that interest turned to love. To Albert's delight, Marie also played the piano, and the two teenagers would often play duets to entertain the other family members. Albert also spent a lot of time playing with the younger Winteler children. He taught them how to make kites out of paper and wood, and then how to fly them. He read to them, sang with them, and even attempted to teach them how to play the violin.

Around this time, Albert recognized that physics might be his true calling. Fascinated by anything that had to do with the science, Albert read every book he could find on the subject and engaged Professor Winteler in discussions about the universe. Albert also realized he could never become an outstanding student by just listening to the required lectures at school. He longed to spend that time in the lab where he could work on experiments, or in the library where he could pursue his research. Fortunately, Albert's best friend and classmate, Marcel Grossman, had the study habits Albert lacked. While Albert worked at the lab or in the library, Marcel took excellent notes at the lectures and shared them with his friend before exams. Albert later wrote, "I would rather not speculate on what would have become of me without those notes!"

During school breaks and vacations, Albert traveled to Italy to visit his parents. On these trips he would keep in close contact with Marie, writing her love letters nearly every day. Their courtship went on until Albert finally graduated from high school and passed the college entrance exam. But their romance ultimately ended when Albert moved to Zurich to attend the Academy.

At the Academy, Albert dove deeper into the world of physics and devoted himself completely to that area of science. He devoured everything, reading the works of great physicists such as Australian-Czech physicist and philosopher Ernst Mach, and great thinkers such as British naturalist and author Charles Darwin. He engaged anyone knowledgeable in physics in lengthy discussions that often lasted well into the night. Albert had many questions about physics, and just as had been the case when he was younger, he could not rest until he found answers.

It was around this time that Albert also began to further question his religious beliefs—specifically, what it meant to be a Jew. It was a confusing time for Albert, living away from his family and his close Jewish friends. With no solid answers, Albert's frustration during that period, led him to eventually sever all ties to the Jewish faith. Years later, he would return to his Jewish roots because of his reaction to the overwhelming anti-Semitism in Germany and his personal involvement with Zionism. Later in his life, in a speech he gave in New York City in 1938, he expressed how important it was for him to acknowledge his Jewish background: "To be a Jew ... means, first of all, to acknowledge and follow in practice those fundamentals in humaneness laid down in the Bible—fundamentals without which no sound and happy community can exist."

During his second year at college, Albert found himself thinking a lot about light, electricity, and the earth's movement. He wondered aloud many times what things might look like if someone were to "go along for the ride on a light wave," keeping pace with it as it traveled though space. He became obsessed with constructing an apparatus that could accurately measure the earth's movement. Little did he know that other, more established theorists were also working on these problems at the same time. Even so, Albert's teachers at the Academy were skeptical and they discouraged him from building this experimental apparatus. Reluctantly, Albert put aside his building plans, but other ideas continued to rage in his mind. He continued to pursue his questions about the nature of heat and electricity.

It soon became obvious to Albert that he was better suited for a career in teaching than as a technical engineer. The more he thought about it, the more the prospect of becoming a physics professor excited him. He turned his energies to passing an upcoming exam that would enable him to become a teacher in Switzerland.

For four years, Albert lived a modest life in the Zurich suburb of Hottingten. He lived in a small room and ate simply, occasionally missing meals altogether. His parents' financial situation had become quite desperate and they could only afford to send him a small amount of money each month. But this was fine with him; he needed very little. Albert had never cared much for nice clothes, fancy dinners, and vacations. When he did have time off from school, he preferred to travel to Milan to see his family. The few costly pleasures he ever allowed himself were tickets to an occasional concert or opera.

Albert continued his studies as a carefree man whose main pleasures in life were playing his music and engaging in heated discussions with friends and fellow students. Early on at the Academy, Albert earned himself the nickname of "the absent-minded professor" because of his forgetful ways and disheveled appearance. His clothes were almost always rumpled and most of the time he never even wore socks!

He was indeed absent-minded. Once, leaving friends after a weekend visit, he forgot his suitcase at their house. His friends said he "will never amount to anything because he can't remember anything!" Often, too, he would forget his house keys and have to wake up his landlady late at night calling, "It's Einstein—I've forgotten my key again!"

4

From Professor to Patents

What is the meaning of human life, or for that matter, of the life of any creature? To know an answer to this question means to be religious. The man who regards his own life and that of his fellow creatures as meaningless is not merely unhappy...but hardly fit for life.

Albert Einstein, 1934

Science without religion is lame, religion without science is blind.

Albert Einstein, 1940

It was in the fall of 1900 that Albert Einstein successfully passed the State examinations at the Confederate Polytechnic Academy at Zurich and became eligible to become a teacher. But what next? There were not many possibilities open to him and he knew he needed to earn money and become self-reliant. He didn't want to keep taking money from his poor parents. Making matters worse, Albert had never become a citizen of Switzerland. In fact, he was not a citizen of any country! Because he was not Swiss, he wasn't permitted to teach in a Swiss school. Plus, he was Jewish, which made getting a teaching position difficult even in Switzerland, which was supposed to be a neutral country that was not known to be as anti-Semitic as Germany.

In 1901, Albert took a substitute position at the Technical School in Winterthur. Because he was only 22 years old, which was young for a teacher, he had trouble at first commanding respect from his students. They sensed his lack of experience and often spoke to each other during his lectures. But eventually, Albert's intelligence and sense of humor won them over. Once he settled into his position, he showed a definite talent for teaching and his students stopped interrupting his lessons and began to show him the proper respect.

Albert lived in a small rented room at the edge of town, with a huge, colorful flower garden right outside his window. He soon discovered that a former classmate from the Academy lived close by and the two joined a local orchestra and played music together every evening. At night, Albert would also continue his scientific research. The teaching position only lasted for a few months and when it was over, Albert again had to look for work. The next opportunity came just in time, for his money had almost run out. He accepted a position tutoring two grammar-school-age boys in the small Swiss city of Rhine. He became friendly with his two students, and again showed a remarkable talent for teaching. But that position also ended after just a few months.

For the third time in his young life, Albert found himself without a job. He turned to his best friend, Marcel

Grossmann, for advice. Marcel spoke to his father about Albert's situation, and his father wrote a glowing letter of recommendation to the director of the Swiss Confederate Patent Office in a city called Bern. (Patents are registrations for new inventions.) The director of the patent office, a man named Friedrich Heller, considered Albert's application with apprehension. While Albert's background in science might be useful at a patent office, Heller knew the young scholar lacked any technical training. Albert's responsibilities would be to write up reports on patent applications—a job that required specific knowledge of engineering. Nevertheless, Heller liked Albert after meeting him and valued the strong recommendation from Marcel's father. He agreed to hire him, and in the fall of 1902, Albert had a new, permanent job.

Albert thoroughly enjoyed his position at the patent office. He worked independently there and received a decent salary. He could now afford his rent and could pay for good meals. While you might think that reviewing patent applications was a lowly position for a physics scholar, Albert never believed the job was beneath him. In fact, Albert considered his position a blessing. Throughout his life, he fondly recalled that his duties at the patent office kept him grounded in reality while still providing him time to work on complex physics problems at home. Later in life, Albert lectured all over the world, often urging young physics students to take what he referred to as a "shoemaker's job" while they studied. He believed that having a job that was "gentle on the brain" was a great way to free development of the creative mind. In his own words, Albert later recalled that his "shoemaker's job" at the patent office provided him with the perfect "opportunity to think about physics."

In Bern, another of Albert's closest friends was a man named Michele (Michael) Besso. Every day after work, the two friends walked home together, discussing everything from nature to physics. Albert called Michele the "best sounding board in Europe" because it was during those long walks that Albert would tell Michele about his theories and ideas and wait anxiously for Michele's comments. Albert and Michele soon found a few more friends who joined them in their discussions. This group of friends met regularly to discuss books on science and philosophy. They playfully called themselves the "Olympia Academy."

Although Albert's work at the patent office was not difficult, it was still tiring. He was not used to sitting for eight hours a day, reviewing papers. Many times he longed to return home to finish working on his research. Often, he tried to accomplish both: If he finished his paperwork quickly, he would use some of the sitting time at the office to work on his personal research. Had the director known about the scraps of paper with math equations scribbled on them that filled Albert's desk drawer at work each day, he probably wouldn't have been too happy about it. But most likely if he had realized that those little paper scraps would soon turn into the most famous scientific theory the world had ever seen, perhaps he wouldn't have minded.

In the spring of 1903, after three years of courtship, Albert married Mileva Maric, a Serbian woman whom he'd fallen in love with in his physics class when he attended the Academy in Zurich. For three years, the two had spent a lot of time apart, with Albert living in Bern and Mileva still in Switzerland. But they kept their romance alive through an exchange of letters every few days. "When you're not with me," Albert wrote to Mileva in 1900, "I feel as though I'm not complete. When I'm sitting, I want to go away; when I go away, I'd rather be home; when I'm talking to people, I'd rather be studying; when I study, I can't sit still and concentrate; and when I go to sleep, I'm not satisfied with the way the day has passed."

Unfortunately, Albert's parents and sister were unhappy about his decision to marry Mileva and expressed their concerns about her to Albert. They believed Mileva was of a lower social class and a bad match for Albert. Albert's father, Hermann, was very sick at the time, suffering from heart disease. He passed away in the fall of 1902, but not before finally relenting and giving Albert his blessing to marry Mileva.

In January, 1903, though none of their family members attended, the two were married in a simple ceremony in Bern. Albert was twenty-three and Mileva was twenty-seven. Afterward, the couple treated their friends Michele Besso, Conrad Habicht, and Maurice Solovine (members of Albert's Olympia Academy) to a celebratory dinner. Albert's friends teased him later when they recalled how he had once again forgotten his house keys on the night of their wedding and had to wake up the landlord.

Albert's salary allowed the couple to live simply in a small top-floor apartment in Kirchenfeld, not far from the patent office. Albert frequently hosted his friends for dinner at the apartment where they discussed physics, politics, and music. It was a lively, happy home, and many times their late-night discussions became so noisy that the downstairs neighbors would complain.

Sadly, it wasn't long before Albert's and Mileva's marriage began to sour. Before they had married, when Albert was working as a substitute teacher, they had learned Mileva was pregnant. But since they were not married at the time, and because Albert had no permanent job and little money, the young couple could not afford to support the child. The painful decision was made to put their daughter, Lieserl, up for adoption. Today, there is no record of what happened to Lieserl, but some historians believe she developed scarlet fever as a baby and died.

Losing her daughter made Mileva depressed and bitter. Soon after they married and moved to Bern for Albert's patent job, the pain became too much for Mileva to bear. Despite the parties and the dinners, life at home became unpleasant for her. Mileva resented having to stay home and take care of the house. She had been a scientist with Albert back at the Academy, and she longed to work, but because she had failed to pass an important test after her graduation, she was unable to get a position at that time. In addition, she often felt ignored by her husband. Albert, she said, always seemed to be ready to discuss everything and anything with his friends, but when it came to her, he was usually quiet and preferred to be left alone.

In Bern, Mileva became pregnant again. This time, she gave birth to a son. Although not a happy couple, the Einsteins were at least better prepared to support a baby. They weren't wealthy by any means but Albert had a steady job, and now that they were married, Albert felt better able to handle the arrival of their baby.

Their son, whom they named Hans Albert, was born in 1904. Young Hans Albert brought much joy to his father. The proud papa could often be found pushing baby Hans Albert—or, Adu as he called him—in a baby carriage through the streets of Bern. These were wonderful times for Albert in spite of his marriage problems with Mileva.

Dividing his time between his job and his family, Albert could barely find time for his research, but he still stayed up well into the night, poring over physics problems that possessed him. Soon a second son was born—Eduard—whom Albert called "Tedel," which means "little bear." Albert helped care for both boys, but his work and research soon began to occupy most of his attention.

5

$$E=mc^2$$

One should not pursue goals that are easily achieved. One must develop an instinct for what one can just barley achieve through one's greatest efforts.

Albert Einstein, 1915

The theory [of relativity] is beautiful beyond comparison. However, only one colleague has really been able to understand it!

Albert Einstein, 1915

During this period of his life Albert Einstein's main efforts in physics were devoted to trying to understand the connection between light, velocity, and motion. Ideas that he had formed back at the Academy, which at that time had been ridiculed by his teachers and he had abandoned for a while, were again at the forefront of his thinking. His days at the patent office were filled with secret problem solving. His nights were spent rocking baby Eduard in his arms while trying to attend to young Hans Albert playing with blocks on the floor by his desk. As Albert tended to the boys, he conducted experiments in his mind, stopping only to write an equation or note on a slip of paper. Albert knew he was close to some answers.

Albert focused mainly on the interaction between light, time, and the earth's electromagnetism and how they all affect matter. Without a laboratory to run experiments, Einstein conducted them in his head, calling them "thought experiments." In these thought experiments he considered how light waves work. He constantly reworked his theories and wrote papers describing his ideas and solutions.

At this time, there were two established theories about the nature of light. Some scientists believed a beam of light was made up of particles, billions of tiny glowing units of energy. Others believed that light was a wave, sort of like the waves in an ocean. The scientists debated and debated, convinced that one of those theories had to be wrong. Waves or particles? Particles or waves? Albert thought they were both right, and he devised mathematical equations to prove that light is both a particle and a wave.

Albert took the study of light one step further, specifically focusing on the speed of light. He realized that nothing can make light speed up or slow down—it always seems to travel at the same speed. He wondered: Is there anything that can affect the speed of light? Perhaps we need to focus on the way we measure it or where we are in space when we see it?

In 1904, Albert had a revelation about light, speed, and time that would change scientific thinking forever. As the story goes, he was riding on a trolley car (a form of public transportation that is like a bus, only it rides along tracks down the middle of busy streets) in

Munich. As the trolley passed the clock tower at the city hall, Albert asked himself, "What time is it?" He realized that he knew the time on the clock because the light had hit the clock face and traveled to his eye. He could see the time. But his eyes had not seen the clock face the instant the light hit it; instead, they had seen the clock's face a few moments after. While the light was traveling to his eye, the trolley was moving away. The second he looked at the clock face, he was actually seeing it a tiny instant later!

Suppose, Albert wondered, the trolley was moving faster and faster? Then that "tiny instant" in time would grow longer. And what if he moved at the speed of light—186,000 miles per second? Of course, he couldn't actually travel that fast ... but suppose he could? Then the light from the clock face would never even reach his eye. This was the type of thought experiment Albert always performed in his mind. This time, however, the more he thought about the clock and the trolley car, the more he believed that the ideas that had been the basis of scientific thinking at that time—the laws and theories for time and light that Sir Isaac Newton had discovered centuries earlier—were wrong. And the more Albert thought about this, the more he began to believe that he was correct. He wondered what would happen if he were to travel at the speed of light and at the same exact moment look at a light wave? Even though the speed of light never changes, would time itself change? Would time stand still? It couldn't!

These ideas were the beginning of Albert's theory of relativity, the theory he later expressed in his most famous equation: $E=mc^2$ (In this equation, the letter **E** stands for "energy"; **m** is for "mass" (which is similar to weight); and c represents "the speed of light" (believed to be the fastest thing in the universe, traveling at a speed of 186,000 miles per second). The word "relativity" refers to the relationship between time, light, motion, and matter. What Albert's equation meant was that in every atom (the "building blocks" of matter comprised of tiny particles called neutrons, protons, and electrons) there was a tremendous amount of energy waiting to be released, and that it was possible to convert atoms into energy and use this energy for big advancements in technology.

More than 2,000 years ago, the Greeks believed the universe was made up of tiny particles called atoms. (You can imagine that atoms look like marbles.) But in the 1800s, scientists began having very different thoughts about atoms. They started to believe that atoms were not solid like marbles, but instead were made up of even tinier particles that were always moving. They thought that these tiny particles moved around something central—much like how the planets in our solar system move around the sun. This central "thing" they called a nucleus. They believed that the particles and the nucleus of the atom were all held together by a gravitational force. These scientists were very determined to learn more about atoms. They felt certain that if they continued to study atoms, they could eventually unlock the mysteries of the universe and reveal how the world worked. But how could they study atoms and particles that were too tiny to even be seen?

Albert didn't let the fact that these atoms could not be seen stop him from studying them. In his thought experiments, he imagined all different scenarios that the atoms would take depending on what he might do to them—if he heated them or if he took away their gravitational force. After considering many, many scenarios, Albert determined that these atoms can be changed into energy. He expressed this idea in his $E=mc^2$. Scientists were intrigued by Albert's ideas and his equation. The more they put his equation to the test, the more they learned that, indeed, great amounts of energy were set free when $E=mc^2$ was applied.

Now that he had completed his thought experiment, Albert began to use mathematical formulas to see what else his discovery revealed about the universe. He soon determined that when two objects are in motion, they have different speeds because of their different masses (weights). Earlier, Sir Isaac Newton believed he had proven that the speed of two objects in motion was the same because the weight differences he was able to measure between the objects were so very small. But what if there was actually a whole world of moving particles that we cannot see with our naked eyes, a world microscopically tiny, where some objects moved at super speeds close to the speed of light? Then we would need a different method of measurement to figure out how these microscopic particles behaved.

Albert was certain that such a world existed and went on to discover this new method of measurement. He published his findings and his equation in a series of scientific papers, and in the process, forever changed the way scientists would view the universe. His equation proved that in every atom there was a tremendous force, an enormous amount of energy waiting to be released.

6

The Papers

The truth of a theory can never be proven; for one never knows if future experience will contradict its conclusions.

Albert Einstein, 1919, "Induction and Deduction in Physics" in the *Berliner Tageblatt* newspaper

Whatever there is of God and goodness in the universe, it must work itself out and express itself through us. We cannot stand aside and let God do it.

Albert Einstein, 1940, Einstein Archives

In March of 1905, at the age of 26, Albert had already published six important papers on intermolecular forces, yet he continued to work in his humble government job—surprising for a man who was about to shake the scientific world.

The importance of Einstein's next paper—the one in which he discussed his new theory of relativity—was not immediately recognized by scientists when it was originally published. First of all, how much could a clerk from the Swiss patent office really know about science? And second, Einstein's ideas were not only difficult to understand, but they completely discredited those of Newton, the recognized authority on such matters. But slowly, scientists began to discuss Albert's theories, and the more they did, the more they realized he was right—and the more they wanted to learn about him.

In fact, as news spread of a great scientist with astounding new theories and ideas, people traveled from all over to the city of Bern to meet the brilliant physicist. Imagine their surprise when they found Albert Einstein worked not at the University, but behind a desk at the Swiss patent office! It was hard for them to believe this young man was the new shining star of the physics world.

Despite his growing fame among the top researchers in his field, Albert still had to make a living. He wanted a teaching job, which had been his earlier plan when he was still a student. Luckily, he found work as a part-time teacher at Bern University. It wasn't a paying position, but one he could manage while still working at the patent office. This was a position that would help him gain the respect he deserved.

One year later, in 1906, Albert had become so well-known and respected that he was offered a teaching position at the University of Zurich. Albert was thrilled by this step up and at age 30 he became an associate professor of theoretical physics. Finally, he was able to resign his position at the patent office.

Being a university professor was very different from being a patent clerk. Albert finally felt treated as an equal by the top scientists in his field. He was invited to meetings where his theories and those of other scientists were discussed. He had the opportunity to perform

Einstein in Berlin, Germany, 1912, where he served as the
director of the Kaiser Wilhelm Institute for Physics.
(Courtesy of the Leo Baeck Institute, New York.)

experiments—not just thought experiments—in real laboratories.

Albert loved lecturing and was a popular professor in Zurich. This was mostly because he was one of the few unconventional professors. He was funny and allowed a casual atmosphere in his classroom. He enjoyed his students and, above all, relished their questions. Remembering his own strict school days in Munich, Albert was determined that his lectures would never be a source of stress and unhappiness for those who attended. He enjoyed spending time with his students outside of the classroom too. Often he could be found dining in cafés after class or bringing groups of students home to discuss the mysteries of the universe over coffee.

Albert found the environment at the University ideal for continuing his work on relativity and began to develop his theories even further. His first theory had had to do with matter in motion—bodies moving at the same time, without changing speeds. This he had called his "special theory of relativity." Now he was eager to find out what would happen to bodies that gained speed as they moved through space. This was to be called his "general theory of relativity," and he would work on this principle for many years to come.

He was also preoccupied with another scientific principle: gravity. Gravity is the force in nature that pulls one object to another. When you toss something into the air, gravity is what pulls it back down to the earth. Albert wondered if gravity could exert this same effect on light. The sun, he knew from earlier experiments performed by scientists, had more gravity than the earth. If this were true, it would mean that the sun's gravity actually pulled on light from distant stars, causing the light to bend.

Unfortunately, Albert had no way of proving if gravity had an effect on light because we can't see starlight when the sun is out and shining.

One day in 1907, Albert had a daydream that helped him form a new theory of gravity. He imagined a crate with no openings, falling freely in space. A man floated in the crate. He was weightless because there is no gravity in space. Albert imagined what would happen if the man dropped a ball as he was floating. The ball would float too. Now, both the man and the ball were weightless. He then imagined that a crane was hooked onto the top of the falling crate. The crane pulled the crate up. Now the man was moving upward. But the force exerted by the crane would act like the force of gravity, Albert imagined, so the man would no longer be weightless. And the ball wouldn't be weightless either.

Albert's thought experiment showed something amazing: that the upward force created by the crane, and the downward force of gravity, both worked in the same way. The upward force of the crane is similar to acceleration or deceleration (the gathering or losing of speed). In this case, the acceleration of the crate created a force that acted like gravity.

Scientists could apply Albert's theory of gravity to what they were learning about space, too. For example, they could use Albert's new formulas to chart the movements of the planets. Previously, scientists had relied on Sir Isaac Newton's formulas for charting the movements of the planets; but Newton's formulas had worked for all the planets except Mercury. Albert's general theory worked for all the planets, Mercury included. Albert's theory further opened up new observations on the relationship between space and time. By applying Albert's theory of relativity, scientists began to wonder if time could be "slowed down" in space. They considered one of Albert's thought experiments called the "twin paradox."

According to the "twin paradox" (which originally began as a thought experiment involving two synchronized clocks, but was later changed to human twins), Albert proposed that if a man flew into space in a rocket traveling near the speed of light and returned, let's say, 50 years later, would he appear to have aged only slightly while his identical twin, who had remained on earth, became old and wrinkled? Albert believed that this is exactly what would take place, because time would slow down for the twin in the rocket.

As a thought experiment, this idea was certainly compelling; but since it could never be proven, many scientists were skeptical. In the case of twins, especially identical twins, it seemed reasonable to assume that their heartbeats were identical and would therefore play the role of the "synchronized clocks" in Albert's original theory. The beats of one twin's heart would indeed slow down relative to the other twin's heart as he or she traveled to space and back. So, even though he could not perform the experiment, the outcome of Einstein's twin paradox appeared to be inescapable: the space-traveling twin would indeed be younger than his stay-at-home brother.

Albert's theories about gravity further introduced scientists to the concept of "black holes" in space. (Black holes are places in space where there is a very strong gravitational pull and no light.) Albert reasoned that if gravity is very strong, even light cannot escape its pull. Time itself stops completely. All that remains is a black hole.

As time went by, Albert became more and more famous. Scientists became convinced about the accuracy of his theories of relativity and the relationship expressed in the formula $E=mc^2$. Offers for teaching positions began to come to him from other universities. At one point, he accepted an offer to teach in Prague, Czechoslovakia. Despite Mileva's protests about leaving Switzerland, the Einsteins moved. Albert spent 18 months in Prague as a professor. This short teaching period in Prague would become a turning point in Albert's life, because it was during that time that he was introduced to the Zionist cause.

For years, Albert's physics research had completely consumed him. He'd had very little time for religion during this period of his life. In fact, up until this time he had all but abandoned his religious beliefs and practices, telling friends that he was less interested in God than finding out the science behind God's creations. He had been almost oblivious to the rising anti-Semitism that surrounded him in the different countries he had lived; but once Albert accepted the teaching position in Prague, he began to feel differently about his faith. The teenager who had thought he could turn his back on Judaism, was now a much wiser man of 30. Although he didn't attend a synagogue or religious services, Albert again felt a connection to the traditions and cultures of Judaism he had learned about as a boy. When he filled out the formal application to the German University in Prague, in the blank space where it asked for the applicant's religion, without hesitation Albert wrote "Jewish."

Albert was anxious to work in Prague for many practical reasons: his salary would be larger, his academic standing at the university would be higher, and his standard of living would be vastly improved. In addition, the German University where he was to teach had one of the best scientific libraries in the world. For Albert, that was the main attraction.

By 1911, Germany was already establishing itself as a military power in Czechoslovakia, and the Czechs resented the Germans for their intrusion into their country. Tension between the Germans and the Czechs grew, and the majority of Czechs were anti-German. Albert had two strikes against him when he arrived in Prague—not only was he considered German (even though he'd renounced his citizenship), but he was also Jewish.

Albert had hoped to push everything from his mind except his work once he took the teaching position in Prague, but it was difficult not to notice that conditions were worsening for the Jews there. He became increasingly sensitive to the strong emotions expressed by his Jewish friends as they gathered together frequently to discuss the Zionist cause. Zionists were Jews from all countries who sought to create a Jewish State (to be called Israel) in Palestine—a place where they could live free from anti-Semitism and prejudice. At that time, Palestine (including the city of Jerusalem) was land controlled by the Ottoman Empire and the Jews who had already settled there were struggling for control of it while battling the Turks and Arabs on an almost daily basis for the right to remain there.

Albert didn't pay too much attention at first to the activities of the Zionists. After all, he was a non-practicing Jew and was way too busy working on his scientific research to pay attention to anything else. Still, he remembered that the Emperor of Czechoslovakia had initially refused to allow him to take his position as a professor because he was Jewish and therefore considered an "unbeliever." Whether he liked it or not, Albert would soon have to deal with the fact that he was a Jew living in an anti-Semitic country.

As he was slowly beginning to reconnect with his Jewish faith, Albert spoke often about his belief in the ideas expressed by Baruch Spinoza—one of the greatest of all modern Jewish philosophers who lived in the 1600s. Spinoza's concept of Judaism rested solely on the idea that nothing in nature is accidental. The philosopher believed strongly in the second commandment, which forbids worshipping God in any image or visible form. The real secrets of nature, Spinoza asserted, couldn't be found by seeing God, but rather by seeing what He has created.

7

Returning to Germany

If God created the world, his primary concern was certainly not to make its understanding easy for us.

Albert Einstein, 1954
Einstein Archives

Mileva Einstein was unhappy living in Prague. She had grown to love Switzerland and uprooting her family to another country had been difficult for her. The move put further strains on their marriage. At the same time, Albert's reputation grew with the spread of his theories throughout the scientific community, and more job offers came pouring in. Universities all over Europe, and even Albert's old school, the Academy in Zurich, asked him to work as a professor there. To have Albert Einstein on your faculty was indeed a big plus.

Although twelve years before the Academy in Zurich had denied Albert a professorship, Albert now chose to accept the Academy's offer, and pretty soon the Einsteins were on the move again, this time back to Switzerland. Mileva was glad to return to Zurich and to her friends after the lonely months she had spent in Prague. But Albert's professorship in Zurich didn't last long. After two years, the Einsteins were on the move again—surprisingly, back to Germany!

Albert was offered a post at the new Kaiser Wilhelm Institute for Physics in Berlin, Germany. In fact, the Kaiser himself (the ruler of Germany at that time) specifically requested that Albert become the institute's director. The director's position was very prestigious. Not only was the salary high, but Albert wouldn't have to teach. Instead, he would oversee the operation of the institute, occasionally address the students, and best of all, he would become a member of the Prussian Academy of Sciences, the most prestigious scientific association in the world.

This offer was difficult to refuse. Not only would the position give him the opportunity to do the theoretical research he never seemed to have enough time to do, but now he would also have all the free time he needed to develop his theories. He would be working in an academic atmosphere among some of the best physicists in the world. This was especially important to Albert because at that time, he was working on some of the most complex aspects of his general theory of relativity. He needed people around him who understood the theory, and most of the scientists who understood relativity were in Berlin.

Still, the job was in Germany. As a schoolboy, Albert had hated the narrow-minded, strict ways of the German teachers in Munich. Berlin, he imagined, would be just as bad. How could he go back? And if he were to take the position, the Kaiser had requested that Albert become a German citizen again.

Albert wanted the position badly, badly enough to pack up his family yet again and move back to the country he had loathed as a child. But this time, Albert decided that should he accept their offer, it would have to be on his terms. First of all, he refused to become a German citizen. He said that he would only accept the appointment if he could be registered as a Swiss citizen and as a Jew. This was a significant position for Albert to take since Jewish citizens in Berlin were being widely persecuted at the time. But Albert remained steadfast. If the Institute wanted him, they would have to take him on his terms— as a Swiss Jew.

The move to Berlin was rough for the Einsteins, especially for Mileva. Everything was different in Berlin—the food, the clothes, the social atmosphere. People were wary of newcomers in Berlin and no one extended any social courtesies to Mileva and her family. She became more and more unhappy and finally decided that she could no longer tolerate the bleak life of Berlin—no matter what her husband's career required. Mileva took the boys and moved back to Switzerland. Officially, Albert and Mileva didn't divorce until many years later, but they never got back together after Mileva's move. Albert remained in Berlin and soon moved into a smaller apartment, alone with his research.

Albert Einstein had never much cared for what other people thought of his appearance or actions. His hair was unruly and he didn't worry if his clothes were wrinkled. When asked what the secret was behind his messy hairdo, he replied, "Neglect!" He could often be seen walking through the University campus in shoes without socks, as had been his habit throughout his life. "When I was young," he once said, "I found out that the big toe always ends up making a hole in a sock. So I stopped wearing socks." Many years later, Albert's secretary, Helen Dukas, revealed in an interview that Albert hadn't even worn socks when he'd visited President Roosevelt in the White House.

Now that he was a bachelor again, Albert cared even less than ever what people thought about him. He seemed to live in his own little world of mathematical formulas. Just as scientists had been surprised to find him wild-haired and unkempt at the Swiss patent office, his reputation continued to remain that of an eccentric: an odd, friendly young man with a hearty, loud laugh— someone who would think nothing of scribbling formulas on a tablecloth at a fancy dinner party or showing up for a meeting in the same clothes he had worn the day before. Albert once joked about his appearance: "It would be a sad situation if the wrapper were better than the meat wrapped inside it." And Albert's usual response to his second wife, Elsa, whenever she urged him to dress properly before going to his office at the University was: "Why should I? Everyone knows me there." And when Elsa tried to insist that he dress appropriately for his first big conference, he replied, "Why should I? No one knows me there."

In Berlin, Albert began to focus on an upcoming solar eclipse that would provide an opportunity for him to test some of his theories. The year was 1914, and Albert had asked his friend Erwin Freundlich to photograph the eclipse in Russia. Albert had been invited on the expedition to Russia by the Imperial Academy of Sciences, but he declined the offer, refusing to visit a country that had persecuted his fellow Jews for so long. So Freundlich packed up his telescopes and cameras and set off for southern Russia to take pictures of the eclipse. Albert was very anxious to see the photos. If they proved that his theories were correct, they would serve as evidence for the entire world to see. If he was wrong, however, he would have to scrap all his work.

During a solar eclipse, the moon passes in front of the sun and blocks the sun's rays. It becomes very dark when this happens (even if it happens in the middle of the day) and the stars come out. If scientists took pictures of the stars that came out during the eclipse, they would be able to see if the gravity from the sun made starlight bend as it passed by.

Unfortunately, Albert's hopes were dashed when Germany declared war against Russia on August 1, 1914—while Erwin and his team were in Russia setting up their equipment. Erwin, who was a German citizen, was captured and put in jail for being on enemy soil! He was released soon after, but the opportunity to photograph the eclipse had come and gone. Testing Albert's theory would have to wait until the next eclipse.

Shortly thereafter, Germany also declared war on France, and then on Belgium. In turn, England declared war on Germany. Albert listened to the news of the war in horror. He despised everything about war and saw reflections of the hated German army from his childhood in the soldiers that were now conquering Europe. The Kaiser, as well as the people of Germany, seemed to want to go to war. To Albert, this was madness. Worst of all, Albert's fellow scientists in Germany were only too eager to help with the German war effort. The Germans had the leading technology in the world and many discoveries for new lethal weapons had been developed by German scientists. They built more weapons than any other nation. They even invented a deadly mustard gas that could be used to kill 5,000 people in just 40 minutes. When he heard this, Albert became enraged.

Albert couldn't sit idly by while his colleagues supported this type of killing. He felt he should take a stand and show the people of the world that there were some scientists in Germany who had not become swept up in the chaos of war. Along with four other peace-seeking professors in Berlin, Albert signed the "Manifesto to Europeans," pleading with sensible citizens and calling for world peace. The "Manifesto" was a statement written by Georg Freidlich Nicholai. Sadly, its message fell on deaf ears.

Life in wartime Berlin was horrible for Albert. At work, his views and his politics set him apart from most of his colleagues. At home, he was lonely, with nobody to help him. He didn't take proper care of himself and pretty soon his friends began to notice he was not sleeping or eating enough. Albert eventually became quite sick with a severe stomach ailment that kept him in bed for months.

Albert missed his sons terribly. Because of the war, border crossings between Germany and Switzerland had become difficult and Albert was unable to visit Hans Albert and Eduard as often as he wanted. Still, he tried to maintain a warm relationship with them. During their separation, he would send toys and write letters to them, promising to visit. His letters were sweet and caring, often reminding them to brush their teeth or practice the piano. "Don't neglect your piano, my Adu," Albert wrote to Hans Albert in 1915, "you don't know how much pleasure you can give to others, as well as to yourself, when you can play music nicely.... Another thing, brush your

Einstein's sons Eduard (left) and Hans Albert in Arosa,
Switzerland, 1917. (Courtesy of the Leo Baeck Institute, New York.)

teeth every day, and if a tooth is not quite all right, go to the dentist immediately. I also do the same and am now very happy that I have healthy teeth." Albert also wrote to his sons of his wish to see them more often and for longer periods of time.

Albert lost 56 pounds during the first two months of his illness. He was literally wasting away and in desperate need of care. Fortunately, living in Berlin at this time were Albert's uncle, his aunt (the sister of his Albert's mother, Pauline), and their daughter, Elsa Lowenthal. When they were children, Elsa and her family would often visit the Einsteins, and she had been one of Albert's and Maja's favorite cousins. "I really delight in my local relatives," Albert wrote in a letter to his friend Paul Ehrenfest, "especially in a cousin of my age, with whom I am linked by an old friendship." Albert remembered Elsa as a happy, kind person, and found this still to be true when she offered to take care of him during his illness.

Recently divorced and with two teenaged daughters of her own—Margot and Ilse—Elsa was happy to nurse her cousin back to health. She cooked and cleaned for Albert, fetched him paper for his notes, and read to him when he was too weak to read. Albert and Elsa became very close during those months, renewing their childhood friendship, and when Albert was finally well, he moved into Elsa's house and became sort of a father to her daughters. When his divorce from Mileva was final in 1919, Albert and Elsa married. "I now have someone about whom I can think with unrestrained pleasure and for whom I can live," Albert wrote to Elsa. "We will give each other the gift of stability and an optimistic view of the world."

Albert knew from the start that he and Elsa were better suited for each other than he and Mileva had been. Unlike Mileva, Elsa had no understanding of physics and she could accept her husband's need for intense study and private thought. "The Lord has put into him so much that's beautiful," Elsa once said of her husband. "I find him wonderful, even though life at his side is enervating and difficult."

8

The Eclipse That Proved it All

If my theory of relativity is proven successful, Germany will claim me as a German and France will declare that I am a citizen of the world. Should my theory prove untrue, France will say that I am a German and Germany will declare that I am a Jew.

Albert Einstein, 1922,
addressing the French Philosophical
Society at the Sorbonne

The value of achievement lies in the achieving.

Albert Einstein, 1950
Einstein Archives

In November of 1918, Germany surrendered to the allied powers—England, France, America, and Russia—and the war was over. Albert was relieved. Now he could return to his work and not worry about the politics of the world around him.

Albert was surprised to learn that while he had been recovering, a copy of his paper on general relativity had been read by a prominent British astronomer and physicist named Sir Arthur Eddington. Though Albert was a German and Eddington an Englishman, Eddington had become very interested in this "enemy" scientist and his theories. He was anxious to photograph the upcoming solar eclipse and put Albert's theory of bending starlight to the test. It would be an opportunity that would not come again for centuries since a solar eclipse of the same magnitude was not due for about another 1,200 years!

The eclipse was due to occur on May 29, 1919, and the only places it would be visible from were South America and Africa. Eddington dispersed teams to both places to take photographs of the stars when the sun was absent. During a total eclipse of the sun, the stars that can not ordinarily be seen because of the sun's powerful light are now visible. If photos are taken of them during an eclipse—when the sun's light is not present—the stars close to the rim of the sun should appear to bend ... according to Albert's theory.

That May, Eddington's teams waited in northern Brazil and on Principe Island in the Gulf of Guinea. They photographed the stars, reset and checked their cameras, then waited for the eclipse. On the morning of May 29, it rained heavily at the African site. The team nearly lost hope that the eclipse would be visible. But at noon, the rain stopped and the sky cleared. As the moon passed in front of the disk of the sun, the photographers snapped away.

It took a few months to compare the photographs of the sky during the eclipse with the photographs of the same part of the sky before the eclipse and after. When

Eddington completed the comparisons, he found that Albert was right. As it turned out, the angle of the starlight was exactly how Albert had predicted it would be. The light from the stars near the sun's rim had "bent" as they passed by the sun. Albert's general theory of relativity had passed an important test.

The news of the eclipse and the success of Albert's theory spread quickly throughout the world. Albert was already a famous figure in the scientific world, but with the world-wide newspaper coverage of the eclipse photos and the account of his proven theory, he became an overnight sensation to common people as well—even to those who had trouble grasping the complicated notion of relativity. The name "Einstein" became known to people throughout the world. Jews everywhere were especially proud that one of their own had been recognized for such an accomplishment!

9

Fame and Fortune

With fame I become more and more stupid, which of course is a very common phenomenon.

Albert Einstein, from *The Human Side*
by Helen Dukas and Banesh Hoffmann

Since the light deflection result became public, such a cult has been made out of me that I feel like a pagan idol. But this, too, God willing, will pass.

Albert Einstein, 1920
Collected Papers of Albert Einstein, Einstein Archives

I have great confidence in a positive development for a Jewish state and am glad that there will be a little patch of earth on which our brethren are not considered aliens.

Albert Einstein, 1919
Collected Papers of Albert Einstein, Einstein Archives

Everyone seemed eager to learn more about Albert Einstein, the "absent-minded professor" who had discredited Sir Isaac Newton. At that time, Newton's theories of gravity were being taught in schools all around the world, so the radical new theory proved by the eclipse was big news. How popular had Albert become? New babies around the world were being named Albert. Newspapers and magazines constantly ran articles and photos of him. "Everything is relative!" became a popular phrase. Few understood what it was and what it meant with regard to our ideas of the universe, but it sounded good nevertheless. Even cartoonists paid Albert a lot of attention drawing funny pictures of an absent-minded professor with Einstein's wild hair. One tobacco company even created a new line of cigars called "The Einstein Cigar!"

Whenever he left the house, Albert was bombarded by photographers and reporters. His phone rang off the hook. Letters by the dozens arrived at his home, from scientists, from universities—even from children looking for help with their math and science homework. Sometimes, the publicity was silly. A popular song came out about the man who "attracted some attention when he found the fourth dimension." Jokes were told about a man who "went out one night at a speed greater than light, and came back the previous day." Albert's and Elsa's peaceful home soon became like a circus and they had to adjust to living with photographers camped outside their door. Albert came to realize that although he wished he could answer every schoolchild who wrote to him, if he did, he would not have time to do anything else.

In 1920, Albert's mother became ill and moved in with Albert and Elsa to spend her remaining days with her son. This time was especially difficult for Albert, watching his mother grow sicker and sicker, but he was glad to spend those last few months with her. After her death later that year, Albert accepted various speaking events that would take him out of Berlin and give him a change of scenery.

Many organizations around the world began to ask Albert to speak at their events. They wanted to hear all about him—his work, his life, his childhood. They all offered him a lot of money to appear. He knew he couldn't possibly speak at every event, so he only replied to the organizations he felt passionate about—groups that shared his views and who would use his appearances and lectures to raise money for important causes. This was how Albert became an active and noble enthusiast for Zionism.

Albert agreed to lecture or appear at all Jewish organizations that asked him. He felt that the persecution of Jews in Germany and throughout Europe demonstrated the need for a Jewish homeland where Jews could find refuge from hatred and prejudice. It had become difficult in Germany and other countries for Jewish students to get accepted at universities and for Jewish professors to get teaching positions. Albert personally knew Zionist pioneers like Chaim Weizmann (who later became the first President of Israel) and he wanted to go a step beyond the establishment of a Jewish homeland. He wanted to help create a Jewish university in Jerusalem— a center of learning where Jews from all over the world would be welcome. So Albert accepted an invitation by Weizmann to help raise money for the Zionist cause and for the creation of a Jewish university that would later become the Hebrew University in Jerusalem. "Zionism really represents a new Jewish ideal," Albert told a friend, "one that can give the Jewish people renewed joy in existence.... I am pleased that I accepted Weizmann's invitation."

Albert Einstein and Chaim Weizmann arriving in New York on the USS Rotterdam, 1921. From left to right: Benzion Mossensohn, Einstein, Weizmann, and Menachem Ussishkin. Mossensohn and Ussishkin were well-known Zionist leaders at that time. (Photograph by Pere Lamiere OP; Courtesy of the Leo Baeck Institute, New York.)

The first stop on this fundraising tour brought Albert and Elsa to America. When the couple arrived by ship, the USS Rotterdam, in New York harbor in April, 1921 they were amazed at the sight that greeted them: Thousands of people had waited for hours to greet the visiting physicist! When they first caught a glimpse of the unkempt Albert standing aboard the incoming ship, holding his pipe in one hand and his violin case in the other, they went wild with cheers and applause.

Usually, when reporters met Albert Einstein, they would ask the same question: "Professor Einstein, can you explain your theory of relativity for our readers?" This day was no different and Albert had his answer already prepared. He stepped off the ship's plank, onto the dock, and said: "The theory shows that time and space are not absolute and exist only where there is matter. Thus, when the universe ceases to exist, time and space will also cease to exist."

Americans fell in love with Albert Einstein, although most of them had no clue as to what his theories were all about. They embraced his casual manner and found him to be soft-spoken, warm, patient, and funny. Albert was a scientist for the people—a regular man, just like them, who just happened to be brilliant. Even his close friend Chaim Weizmann joked about Albert and his hard-to-grasp equation. "During our crossing," Weizmann is reported to have said after they arrived in New York, "Einstein explained his theory to me every day, and by the time we arrived I was fully convinced he understood it."

On this trip, Albert had traveled to the United States with a group of Zionist leaders (led by Weizmann). Together, they were to take a six week coast-to-coast tour to promote the cause of a Jewish national homeland and to raise funds for the establishment of a Jewish university in Jerusalem. "I know of no public event that has given me such pleasure as the proposal to establish a Hebrew University in Jerusalem," Albert said in an interview with *The New York Times* newspaper during the trip. "The traditional respect for knowledge that Jews have maintained intact through many centuries of severe hardship has made it particularly painful for us to see so many talented sons of the Jewish people cut off from higher education."

Addressing the thousands at New York harbor, Chaim Weizmann said: "Professor Einstein has done us the honor of accompanying us to America in the interest of the Hebrew University of Jerusalem. Zionists have long cherished the hope of creating in Jerusalem a center of learning in which the Hebrew genius shall find full self-expression and which shall play its part as interpreter between the Eastern and Western worlds." Albert envisioned the Hebrew University as the institution where Jewish scholars who had been fired from their positions in their own countries simply because they were Jews could come and study, free from persecution. "I have warm sympathy for the affairs of the new colony in Palestine," Albert told the World Zionist Organization, "and especially for the yet-to-be-founded university. I shall gladly do everything in my power for it."

This visit to the United States, his first trip outside Europe, made a lasting impression on Albert. He was received everywhere as a hero. Thousands of American Jews greeted him with cheers, with American flags, and with blue and white flags of the Zionist movement. He was escorted in a motorcade from New York harbor to City Hall, and he had official escorts in every city he visited. *The New York Times* reported on his visit to Cleveland on May 25th of that year: "He was greeted by a near riot of fan frenzy, a military band, and a motorcade of two hundred cars. He was saved from possibly serious injury only by strenuous efforts of a squad of Jewish war veterans who fought the people off in their mad efforts to see him."

Years later, Albert wrote: "It was in America that I first discovered the Jewish people. I have met Jews, but the Jewish people I met were either in Berlin or elsewhere in

Germany. These Jewish people I found in America came from Russia, Poland, and Eastern Europe generally.... I found these people extraordinarily [self-sacrificing]. They have, for instance, managed in a short time to secure the future of the [upcoming] university in Jerusalem."

Before leaving the United States, Albert was honored at a gala dinner at the Waldorf Astoria Hotel in New York City. It was sponsored by the American Jewish Physicians Committee—the forerunner of today's American Friends of The Hebrew University—and attended by 800 Jewish doctors. They were inspired by Einstein's speech to fund the university's first medical sciences laboratory and to purchase additional land on Mount Scopus in Jerusalem. On that single evening, they raised $250,000!

Albert and Elsa next traveled to the other side of the world to visit Japan and other Asian countries. They were always greeted in the same way—showered with praise and honors. En route to Japan in 1921, Albert learned he'd been awarded the Nobel Prize for physics for his earlier work on the photoelectric effect that showed light was both a particle and a wave. The Nobel Prize was, and still is, one of the most prestigious awards in the world. In fact, Albert had previously been nominated for the Nobel Prize for Physics eight times, but had never won.

Everyone thought it was odd that Albert, who was regarded as the greatest scientist of the time, had never won the Nobel Prize for Physics. During the years he was nominated, there were two years that the prize wasn't awarded to anyone, so his not having won was a mystery. After his win in 1921, an author named Irving Wallace (who was writing a book about the Nobel Prize) decided to investigate why Einstein hadn't won for so many years. Wallace learned that one of the Nobel Prize judges was a German scientist named Phillip Lenard. Lenard, who was an anti-Semite, had great influence over all the other judges. From 1910 to 1921, Lenard had pressured the committee not to award Albert the prize even though most of them felt he deserved it. By 1922, Lenard's influence had worn thin and that, combined with the fact that Albert was now a world-famous figure, enabled the committee to award him the prize he had deserved for so long.

Albert was excited and honored to have won. Not only did the Nobel Prize come with fame and recognition, it came with what was a great fortune at the time—$32,500. Albert quickly arranged to have all the prize money sent to Mileva to provide for her and their two sons. He finally felt relieved to know that she and the boys would always be well cared for.

On their way home from Japan, Albert and Elsa stopped in Palestine (now Israel), Albert's first trip to the future Jewish homeland was an emotional and exciting experience—a chance to see firsthand the land and the people he was so passionately speaking for. In a sense, it was a defining moment for the man who had once renounced his faith. "So long as I lived in Switzerland, I did not become aware of my Jewishness," Albert said in an article in *The Jewish Review* in 1921 entitled "How I Became a Zionist." "This changed as soon as I took up residency in Berlin. I saw how anti-Semitism prevented Jews from pursuing orderly studies and how they struggled to secure a livelihood. What one must be thankful for to Zionism," he added, "is that it is the only movement that has given Jews a justified sense of pride."

Albert Einstein with an unidentified group of Zionist supporters during a trip to Haifa, Palestine (Israel), 1923. (Courtesy of the Leo Baeck Institute, New York.)

The Einsteins sailed to Haifa, a city in northern Palestine, and then visited the palatial home of Herbert Samuel, Palestine's British high commissioner. On February 7, 1922, Albert was officially welcomed by the Palestine Zionist executive. The next morning, he and Elsa were driven through streets lined with cheering schoolchildren to a reception in his honor at the Lemel School, one of the first modern schools in Jerusalem. Albert spoke to the crowd of people at the school, proclaiming it to be "the greatest day of my life. This is a great age, the age of the liberation of the Jewish soul; and it will be accomplished through the Zionist movement, so that no one will be able to destroy it."

The highlight of Albert's 12-day tour was when he spoke on Jerusalem's Mount Scopus, where plans were in motion to build the Hebrew University. There, on February 9, Albert inaugurated the institution that he had helped make possible through his tireless fundraising efforts and vocal support for the Zionist cause. At a British police academy hall on Mount Scopus, he delivered the University's first-ever scientific lecture. The event was chaired by the Zionist leader Menachem Ussishkin, who concluded his introductory remarks by saying: "Professor Einstein, please rise to the podium that has been waiting for you [for] two thousand years." Einstein began his lecture in Hebrew and then apologized for being unable to continue in the language of his own people, and resumed his speech in French, the more common language spoken in Palestine at the time.

In Palestine, Albert continued his tour, touring the cities of Haifa and Tel Aviv and then visiting a collective farm community called a "kibbutz." He was very impressed with the spirit of the Jewish pioneers everywhere he went. He could now believe that a Jewish State was most definitely on the horizon. "By repatriating Jews to Palestine and giving them a healthy and normal economic existence," Albert said in "How I Became a Zionist" in 1921, "Zionism ... enriches human society." When it was time to return home, Albert told Chaim Weizmann, "The difficulties here are great, but the mood is confident and the work to be marveled at."

Albert's last stop was Sweden where he spoke before 2,000 people—including the King of Sweden—and officially accepted his Nobel Prize. While Albert was aware of the prestige that came with the award, he was not about to put on airs for anybody... even a king! So when he arrived at the dinner ceremony in an old suit jacket that had seen better days and was offered a clean, new jacket, he refused it. He simply brushed his own, rumpled jacket sleeve with his hand and said, "We can put a sign on my back: 'This suit has just been brushed.'" Albert remained true to his unique personality—always the down-to-earth, absent-minded professor!

As their world tour came to an end, Albert and Elsa felt wonderful about all the attention they had received, how people had welcomed them with open hearts and open arms wherever they went. But upon their return to Germany, everything began to change.

10

Anti-Semitism at Home

Perhaps it is due to anti-Semitism that we can preserve ourselves as a race: at least, this is what I believe.

Albert Einstein, 1920
from a German newspaper article

The Germans were still bitter over their defeat in World War I. The country had spent a great deal of money and resources fighting the war and its citizens were growing desperate because they couldn't find jobs or a way to provide for their families. The people looked for someone to blame for their hardships. They believed that those who refused to help with the war effort were the cause for their misfortunes, especially the Jewish people. Albert fit both descriptions: he had been vehemently opposed to the war, and he was Jewish. He, and the Jewish people as a whole, became the scapegoats (someone to blame) for Germany's post-war problems.

Albert visit with his sons, Eduard (left) and Hans Albert, on the balcony of Mileva Maric's home in Zurich, Switzerland, 1924. (Photograph by Armin Harmann; Courtesy of the Leo Baeck Institute, New York.)

In Berlin, citizens would often gather to publicly discuss their economic frustrations. These meetings quickly turned into hate-fests where anti-Semitic speakers and leaders would say terrible things about the Jews and denounce Albert and his theories. They even went so far as to say that no Jewish person could ever have developed a successful physics theory as Albert had. They claimed that only "Aryan" minds could think like that. Albert's theories were dismissed as "Jewish physics." (In Nazi racial theory, Aryans were people of pure German "blood." The term "non-Aryan" was used to designate Jews, part-Jews, and others of supposedly inferior racial stock.)

Albert knew that the attacks on him and his work were unfounded. He knew that great minds across the world had tested and proved his theories, so he did his best to ignore the attacks. But as meeting upon meeting was called to discuss what to do about him, he soon began to feel that his life was in danger. Rumors started to circulate about an assassination attempt on his life for disgracing the German people, and Albert became more worried. This was shocking, especially since he had just brought so much honor and pride to Germany by his winning the Nobel Prize.

In Munich—Albert's hometown—the atmosphere was turning dangerous too. A man named Adolph Hitler was gaining the support of the German people, appealing to their fears that the Jews were responsible for all their money woes. He formed the Nazi party—a radical movement aimed at gaining control of Germany. The Nazi party began small, but later grew to become a major political force.

It was a strange time for Albert, attacked in his own country and praised almost everywhere else in the world. But despite the continued political rallies—and even an "anti-Einstein" rally held in Berlin—Albert did his best to continue with his work. He was beginning work on a new theory—the unified theory—one that would explain the relationship between other forces of nature. It was a huge task—one that he would work on for the rest of his life. He was also embroiled in a bitter battle with a Danish scientist named Niels Bohr over theories in quantum physics (the study of atoms, matter, and energy and their relation to the workings of the universe). This battle would rage for years in the scientific world.

During this time, Albert got away from Berlin as much as possible. He would often take the ten-hour train ride from Berlin to Zurich to see Hans Albert and Eduard. Hans Albert told his father that he hoped to become an

Albert, Elsa, and Margot Einstein in their home in Berlin, Germany, 1929. (Photograph by Armin Harmann; Courtesy of the Leo Baeck Institute, New York.)

engineer when he grew up. Eduard's future, unfortunately, seemed much more uncertain. Eduard had shown signs of mental illness as he grew older, and Albert was worried about him. But he was proud of his younger son's passion for learning and his excellent memory.

Albert also took a month's vacation to Holland to stay with his good friend Paul Ehrenfest. The Ehrenfests set up a small table for him in their dining room and had milk, bread, cheese, and cakes always available for him. They gave him a quiet place to work and a cozy bed to sleep on. Of course, Albert had his violin too. He often proclaimed that in Holland he had everything he needed. "What more can a man want?" he asked.

It was while on vacation in Holland that Albert first read about Adolf Hitler and the Nazis. During a political rally in Munich, Hitler had jumped up onto a table and fired his revolver to get attention. "The National Revolution has begun!" he shouted. He held people at gunpoint and threatened to kill them if they didn't join his party. The next morning, Hitler and his Nazi soldiers smashed the printing machines of a Democratic newspaper called the *Social Democrat* and seized the office of the War Ministry. Three thousand Nazi soldiers in brown uniforms marched toward Munich's center. Germany was changing right before Albert's eyes. In Vienna, Austria at the time, Albert was interviewed by a reporter about the situation in Germany. "Doesn't the world see that Hitler is aiming for war?" he asked the reporter.

As he aged, Albert Einstein continued to make contributions to physics, but those contributions lacked the magic and brilliance of his earlier work. He went on to publish papers on his unified theory, but he never succeeded in finishing the theory. In 1929, the long years of hard work, exhaustion, and poor health habits caught up with Albert. One day, while carrying a heavy suitcase through the snow, he collapsed. His doctor diagnosed a weak and infected heart. It took Albert a full year of rest to recuperate, but he was never really himself again. Still, he continued his work, usually within the quiet, undisturbed peace of his bedroom. Sadly, it was from that bedroom window that Albert watched the Nazi soldiers as they paraded their messages of hate to the desperate German people. Albert knew that despite the peace of his bedroom, the old German madness was on the rise again.

11

The Philanthropist

Zionism strengthens the self-confidence of Jews, which is necessary for their existence in the Diaspora, and a Jewish center in Palestine creates a strong bond that gives Jews moral support.

Albert Einstein, 1921
"How I Became a Zionist," in *The Jewish Review*

Germany had the misfortune of becoming poisoned, first because of plenty, and then because of want.

Albert Einstein, 1923
Einstein Archives

Caring for Albert took its toll on Elsa. She had become Albert's nurse, housekeeper, secretary, and business manager. After several days, Albert noticed her exhaustion and agreed that they should hire a secretary. A close friend of Elsa's recommended her sister, Helen Dukas, for the position. Helen had just lost her job at a publishing company and was available. Helen Dukas was a tall, lively, attractive woman. Albert and Elsa liked her from the start and hired her immediately. Helen ended up working as Albert's secretary until his death in 1955. Her job, she explained, was to cook and to attend to Albert's mail. She ultimately became a loving friend and confidant as well.

Albert recuperated at home for nearly a year after his collapse. He later admitted that his illness turned out to be a blessing. At home, with no distractions, he was able to continue with his work on unified theories in physics. When he felt well enough, he resumed his position at the Kaiser Wilhelm Institute, meeting with colleagues all morning, then resting after lunch. Helen remembers he would work through the night on occasion, his only means of sustenance a bowl of his favorite pasta—macaroni—for dinner.

Despite his difficult recuperation and the demands of his return to work, Albert always made sure to help people in need. While he refused interviews with the press and most speaking engagements, he tried to reply to the needy people who wrote to him. Most of the time these letters were from children, and often, many were from fellow Jews all over the world asking for help.

One such Jew was a man named Phillipe Halsman. Albert received a letter from Halsman's sister explaining that her brother was being held in an Austrian prison for killing their father. Phillipe was innocent, his sister wrote, and in prison only because he was Jewish. After learning the details of the case through Halsman's sister, Albert wrote to the Austrian president, Wilhelm Miklas, on behalf of Phillipe Halsman. Even though there were demonstrations in Austria demanding Halsman's release, it was Albert's letter that got the job done. The Austrian president freed Phillipe from jail. Phillipe moved to Paris and started a new life as a photographer. He was always eternally grateful to Albert. A few years later, he joined Albert in the United States and photographed him. One of his photos was used later on a United States postage stamp honoring the physicist. Albert was forever proud to have helped free an innocent man from prison.

As life for the Jews of Germany became increasingly difficult, Albert became even more sympathetic to the political ideas of Zionism and was determined to work toward the one goal in his life that mattered more than physics: creating a Jewish State. When he was well enough, he decided, he would tour the world again and ask for both financial and public support. "Zionism, to me," he had written a few years earlier in *The Jewish Review*, "is not just a colonizing movement to Palestine. The Jewish nation is a living fact in Palestine and in the Diaspora [outside of Palestine], and Jewish feelings must be kept alive wherever Jews live. I believe that every Jew has duties toward his fellow Jews."

In 1929, Albert celebrated his 50th birthday in Berlin. His birthday was recognized as a major event around the world. In Palestine, Albert learned they had planted a forest in his name. He received thousands of birthday cards, including cards from the king of Spain, the emperor of Japan, and the president of the United States, Herbert Hoover. He also received gifts from all over the world: violins, tobacco, art, and food. The mayor of Berlin held a reception for Albert and Elsa in honor of his birthday and decided the city would present Albert with a summer home as a gift. Plans were underway to build a house for the Einsteins in the lake resort of Caputh in Germany. Unfortunately, not everyone in Berlin was happy to reward "a Jew" on his birthday, and after much discussion, the gift was canceled. Albert and Elsa liked the idea

of a summer home and decided to build the house themselves in the quiet, lakeside resort. The Einsteins spent
the next four summers in Caputh. Their new house sat
atop a hill among the pine trees, with magnificent views
of the village and lakes below. Some of Albert's wealthier
friends bought him a sailboat for his birthday, and Albert
spent nearly every day sailing with Elsa, Margot, and
Ilse, or with visiting friends and relatives. His first sailing
guest in Caputh was his son, Hans Albert. On the days
he didn't sail, Albert hiked and enjoyed other outdoor
activities.

Albert especially loved his private bedroom in Caputh,
with its custom-built desk and storage space for his violin. From his desk he had wonderful views of the lakes.
Above his bookshelf he hung his favorite portrait of Sir
Isaac Newton and a photograph of his sons. Caputh
became Albert's paradise, the perfect escape from the
hustle and bustle of Berlin and the constant demands of
the public. In Caputh, Albert could pursue his work and
enjoy his free time in quiet seclusion.

The Einsteins welcomed many visitors to their summer home—friends from Berlin, family members such as
Maja, Hans Albert, and Eduard, and fellow Nobel Prize
laureates. The Einsteins also enjoyed visits from Chaim
Weizmann and Albert's friends from the Olympia Academy. Albert and Elsa had two pets at their summer home:
a long-haired dachshund named Purzel and a stray cat
named Peter. Albert took long walks with Purzel and
spent hours working at his desk with Peter at his feet.

It was in Caputh where Albert developed an intense
passion for sailing. His sailboat, which he named "Tüm-
mler" (a Yiddish word that translates best into English as
"moving and making a lot of noise"), had two sleeping

Einstein pursuing one of his favorite pastimes—sailing—at his vacation home in Caputh, Germany, 1935. (Hebrew University of Jerusalem Albert Einstein Archives—Courtesy of AIP Emilio Segre Visual Archives.)

compartments and was considered quite luxurious. On his quiet sailboat Albert often found the peace and relaxation he needed, but just in case an idea or inspiration came while out on the lake, he always made sure that he had pencils and paper on board.

When the Einsteins moved to Caputh for the summer of 1929, Adolph Hitler and the Nazi party were already on their way to controlling the people and government of Germany. The political party Hitler started in Munich back in 1923 had grown very strong. Hitler and the Nazis were determined to turn all of Germany against the Jews.

Albert continued his efforts to raise money for a Jewish homeland and for the Hebrew University. He felt now, more than ever, the Jews needed his help. "Jewry has proved throughout history that the intellect is the best weapon," he said in an address at a Jewish meeting in Berlin at the time. "It is our duty as Jews to put at the disposal of the world our several-thousand-year-old sorrowful experience and, true to the ethical traditions of our forefathers, become soldiers in the fight for peace."

In the following year, he appeared at a fundraiser in a Berlin synagogue. Wearing a black *kippah* (the Hebrew word for a skullcap), Albert gave a concert for the congregation on his violin. Soon after, he traveled to London to help raise money for European Jews to go to Palestine. As the guest of honor at a banquet in London, Albert spoke to thousands in attendance and his words were broadcast by radio to Germany and the United States. "The Jewish national home is not a luxury," he said, "but a necessity for the Jewish people." Later that year, in the United States, Albert celebrated Hanukkah with 15,000 Jews at Madison Square Garden in New York. Again, he urged

Einstein with his secretary Helen Dukas a charity concert at the New Synagogue Oranienberger Strasse, Berlin, 1930. Albert played pieces on his violin by composers Bach and Handel. (Photograph by Dr. Eric Salomon; Courtesy of the Leo Baeck Institute, New York).

them for their support. He was also honored at Columbia University, where they played "Hatikvah" (The future Jewish national anthem) before he spoke.

By 1933, the Nazis controlled political life in Germany. Albert was often the target of verbal abuse and his theory of relativity was denounced by the Nazis as "Jewish-Communist physics." Being both Jewish and a pacifist, Albert was subject to Nazi ridicule. A pamphlet was even printed and signed by many German scientists condemning his ideas. Life for the Jewish citizens of Germany became intolerable and Albert knew that the time would soon come when he would be forced to leave Germany forever. In the spring of 1932, Albert resigned from his position at the Kaiser Wilhelm Institute. When asked about his reason for leaving he said, "I did not wish to live in a country where the individual does not enjoy equality before the law and freedom to say and teach what he likes."

That summer in Caputh, a family friend confided to Elsa that the commander-in-chief of the German army had advised her to warn all her Jewish friends to leave Germany—especially Albert Einstein. So, at the end of the summer in 1932, Albert and Elsa left Caputh and headed for the United States, where he was to embark on a lecture tour. As he prepared for the trip, Albert turned to Elsa and said, "Before you leave our villa this time, take a close look. You'll never see it again."

Sadly, Albert had been right. While the Einsteins were in America, Hitler was appointed Reich Chancellor of Germany and immediately demanded a boycott of Jewish businesses in the country. Albert's summer house in Caputh and all its belongings were seized by the Nazis. His apartment in Berlin was also confiscated, as German Jews were now forbidden to own property. "I have now been promoted to being an evil monster in Germany, and all of my money has been taken away," Albert wrote to his friend Max Born, after his German bank account had been confiscated. "But I console myself with the thought that it would soon have been spent, anyway."

Even more frightening, Einstein's published writings—his papers, theories and books—were all publicly burned. His precious sailboat was taken away and there was even a reward announced for his capture. Luckily, Elsa's daughter, Margot, managed to smuggle most of Einstein's important papers out of Germany before the Nazis could find them.

Albert and his family decided to remain in the United States. He accepted a job at the Institute for Advanced Study in Princeton, New Jersey. He cut off all contacts with every German institution he had ever dealt with. He would never again return to Germany. "As long as it is possible for me," he said, "I will only stay in a country in which political freedom, tolerance and equality of all citizens is stated in the law."

Always the humanitarian, Albert spent much of his time in the United States helping those less fortunate than he. Of course, his major interest was Zionism, but he also felt compelled to act on the behalf of individuals or groups of people who needed help. In 1931, while still living in Germany, he had joined an international protest to save the lives of eight African-Americans in Scottsboro, Alabama who had been wrongly imprisoned. In 1932, along with famous psychologist and fellow Jew, Sigmund Freud, Albert published an anti-war pamphlet entitled, "Why War?" In 1933, he met with England's Prime Minister, Winston Churchill, and prominent British scientists and intellectuals to warn them about the danger posed by the Nazis.

What became Albert's ultimate goal during the following years, however, was his effort to rescue as many Jews as possible from the deadly peril they faced in Germany. After just three years of Nazi rule, Hitler's campaign against the Jews had intensified. Signs over doorways to some stores read, "Jews not admitted." Towns in Germany had signs posted, "Jews strictly forbidden in this town," or "Jews enter this place at their own risk." In some communities, Jews couldn't enter a store to buy milk or medicine for their families.

Albert did whatever he could to help smuggle Jews out of Germany. He wrote letters to the President of the United States, asking for his help. He signed affidavits and auctioned off personal possessions to raise money. He even lied, claiming people were relatives when they were not, just to get them the necessary papers to get out of Germany. Many times his efforts were rewarded, and Jews were let go. Other times, there was nothing Albert could say or do to free his fellow Jews. These failures deeply saddened the famous scientist, but increased his determination to try to stop the Nazis persecution of Jews.

12

Einstein at Princeton

There are no German Jews, there are no Russian Jews, there are no American Jews. Their only difference is their daily language. There are in fact only Jews.

Albert Einstein, 1935
in a Purim dinner speech in the United States

Albert and Elsa were happy in their new home in Princeton, New Jersey. Helen Dukas, Albert's secretary, moved with them, as did Elsa's daughters Margot and Ilse and their families. By then, Albert's sons, Hans Albert and Eduard, were grown men. Hans Albert had married and had children of his own. He and his family left Zurich, Switzerland in 1938 and emigrated to the United States, first to South Carolina and then to California. Hans Albert had followed in his father's footsteps and had become a professor of engineering.

Albert's son Eduard had the misfortune of suffering from a severe mental illness that caused him to become institutionalized in Switzerland for most of his adult life. Before that time, he had studied medicine, hoping to become a psychiatrist. But in his mid 20s his health deteriorated. He lived in the Zurich institution until his death in 1965.

The Einsteins' first two years in Princeton, New Jersey, were spent in a two-family house at 2 Library Place. By 1935, Albert had made the decision to live in the United States permanently. He began the formal process of obtaining residency and citizenship. (He would finally become as United States citizen in 1941.) In the fall of 1935, he and Elsa moved to a white, two-story house at 112 Mercer Street, which would become their permanent home . The park-like grounds at Princeton University and the beautiful ivy-covered old buildings provided an ideal atmosphere for Albert. He and his family quickly became part of the local community, which was proud to welcome the esteemed physicist. Albert and Elsa lived on Mercer Street for the remainder of their lives, along with a dog named Chico, a cat named Tiger, and later, a parrot named Bibo.

The Einsteins adjusted quite nicely to life in America, though it was difficult to forget the terrors that were raging back in Germany. Albert watched and listened to the news in horror as the Nazis continued to persecute Jews. Albert had always prided himself on being a pacifist—someone who was totally against war. But now, he felt as if he could no longer be a pacifist. He knew that Hitler and the Nazis had to be stopped and that other countries would have to go to war in order to stop them.

Albert became alarmed when he learned that the Nazis had invaded Czechoslovakia. He knew that the Czechs had uranium, and believed that the Nazis would use the uranium to build nuclear weapons. With their deep hatred of Jews, he feared the Nazis would use those deadly weapons on the Jews or on any of their enemies—including the United States.

Albert knew the only way he might possibly make a difference was by using his fame and influence, so he decided to write a letter to the President of the United States, who at that time was Franklin D. Roosevelt. In it, he tried to convince Roosevelt that America needed to develop a powerful defense against the Nazis. An atomic bomb, he said, could and should be built, using his research. Albert also found another way to use his fame to support the United States in the war effort. He hand-wrote his famous theory of relativity and auctioned it off to the highest bidder. It sold for an incredible six million dollars and it now resides in the Library of Congress.

Albert's theory, $E=mc^2$, did not lead directly to the building of the atomic bomb, but its formula suggested that breaking apart the atom would release a great deal of energy. The formula was ultimately used by others in efforts to create explose devices. President Roosevelt organized a team of scientists and set up the "Manhattan Project," a top secret research facility in New Mexico, where scientists and physicists could work on making an atomic bomb.

Because of Albert's letter to President Roosevelt, Albert became known as "the father of the atomic bomb." But this "honor" turned out to be a terrible thing for Albert. When he finally learned that Germany had actually not been able to make much progress building their bomb, he regretted ever writing the letter. The thought that his formula could result in the killing of innocent people deeply troubled him. In 1945 he again wrote to President Roosevelt—this time begging him not to use the bomb. Unfortunately, President Roosevelt died before receiving

Albert's letter. When the next President, Harry S. Truman, ordered the use of the atomic bomb during wartime, Einstein felt horribly responsible for the massive destruction and loss of lives the bombs had caused. "Had I known that the Germans would not succeed in producing an atomic bomb, I never would have lifted a finger," Albert told a *Newsweek* magazine reporter in 1947.

13

The End

The support for cultural life is of primary concern to the Jewish people. We would not be in existence today as a people without this continued activity in learning.

Albert Einstein, 1950
The New York Times

Subtle is the Lord, but malicious he is not.

Albert Einstein quote
engraved above a fireplace at the faculty lounge of
the Mathematics Department at Princeton University

From Princeton, Albert traveled one last time to Europe—to Switzerland to visit his son Eduard. Eduard, Mileva wrote, was having a very difficult time at the Zurich mental institution to which he had been committed. During his visit, Albert stayed with Eduard, playing soothing concerti at night for his son on the violin. Sadly, this was the last time he would see Eduard—or Mileva—again. Albert kept in close contact with his Hans Albert while living in Princeton, and was thrilled when his son and grandchildren visited him from California.

In 1936, Elsa Einstein passed away. Albert was surrounded by family during this difficult time—Elsa's
daughters and Helen Dukas were all living at 112 Mercer
Street then—and Albert sought comfort and solace from
them. Helen Dukas took charge of the household after
Elsa's death, tending to all the cooking, cleaning, and
business.

In 1939, Albert's sister Maja came to live with her
brother in Princeton. Albert was completely devoted to
his sister, who lived with him from 1939 until her death
in 1951. After she became bedridden from a stroke, Albert
stayed by her bedside, reading to her every single night.
A close family friend commented on the loving relationship between Albert and Maja in their old age. "These
two old people," she said, "were always sitting together
with their bushy hair, in complete agreement, understanding, and love." Albert devoted most of his time in
Princeton to his scientific work, but found time to enjoy
sailing on Princeton's beautiful Lake Carnegie in his boat
called "Tinnet," which means "cheaply made" in Yiddish.
Of course, he was still passionate for music and became
a well-known figure walking through campus with his
shocking-white hair, shoes with no socks, and violin case
tucked under one arm. He played for students, faculty,
and anyone who would ask!

When World War II was finally over in 1945, in addition to all his efforts in supporting the establishment of
the State of Israel, Albert also spoke out for world peace.
He even went so far as to promote his ideas for a unified "world government" (all countries would become
united under one government). He urged nations to
disarm. His hope was that with no armed forces and
fewer governments making the rules, there would be

Albert Einstein and Israeli Prime Minister David Ben-Gurion, 1951. Ben-Gurion asked Einstein to become the president of Israel, but he did not accept the offer. (Hebrew University of Jerusalem Albert Einstein Archives—Courtesy of AIP Emilio Segre Visual Archives.)

fewer reasons for countries to go to war. It was a concept that sounded good in theory, but one that was never accepted by many people.

Albert also continued to speak out against Germany. Along with some of his relatives who had been murdered by the Nazis in Italy, three of his cousins who had remained in Germany perished in German death camps. Albert grieved for all Jews who had perished at the hands of Nazis. "The Germans slaughtered my Jewish brethren," he said. "I will have nothing further to do with them."

In 1948, Albert, along with the rest of the world, saw the creation of the Jewish State. The previous November, the United Nations had voted to support the division of Palestine between Arabs and Jews. Six months later, on May 14, 1948, the first Prime Minster of Israel, David Ben-Gurion, addressed the world by radio as the Tel Aviv Philharmonic played "Hatikvah." "The State of Israel has come into being!" he said. In Princeton, Albert celebrated. He called the event, "the fulfillment of our dreams." The following November, he gave an address on the radio for the United Jewish Appeal. "The Jews of Palestine," he said in a proud voice, "did not fight for political independence for its own sake, but they fought to achieve free immigration for the Jews of many countries where their very existence was in danger; free immigration also for all those who were longing for a life among their own. It is no exaggeration," he added, "to say that they fought to make possible a sacrifice that is perhaps unique in history."

In 1952, Albert's friend and the first president of Israel, Chaim Weizmann, died. Shortly after Weizmann's death Albert received a letter from Prime Minister David Ben-Gurion asking him to become the next president of Israel. Albert didn't think that he was up for the challenge. At 73, he was finally at peace in Princeton. He knew he was not a politician. And though he still worked tirelessly to support the new Jewish homeland, Albert's first true love was for science. He decided to refuse the offer and remain in Princeton, doing what little research he could at this late stage of his life. "I am deeply moved by the offer of Israel," he wrote back to Ben-Gurion, "and at once saddened and ashamed that I cannot accept it." He also wrote in a statement to Abba Eban, Israel's ambassador to the United States, "Ever since I became fully aware of our precarious situation among the nations of the

Albert Einstein at his home in Princeton, New Jersey, a few months before his death in1954. (Hebrew University of Jerusalem Albert Einstein Archives—Courtesy of AIP Emilio Segre Visual Archives.)

world, my relationship to the Jewish people has become my strongest human bond."

In 1955, Albert was rushed to a hospital emergency room after complaining of stomach pains. A few days later, on April 18, the scientist who had revolutionized science, died of an aneurysm of his abdominal aorta—

Albert Einstein's last blackboard in his study at the Institute for Advanced Study, Princeton University, 1955. (Hebrew University of Jerusalem Albert Einstein Archives—Courtesy of AIP Emilio Segre Visual Archives.)

one of the large arteries that carried blood to and from his heart had burst. In accordance with Albert's wishes, his body was cremated. He had arranged to have his brain preserved for future scientific research. His money, important papers, letters, notes, and belongings were left to the Hebrew University in Jerusalem under the care of Helen Dukas.

Science had lost one its most important figures; the world had lost a prominent physicist; and the Jews of the world had lost a fighter for peace and a hero who had defended freedom and justice.

THE EINSTEIN PAPERS

This life is not such that we ought to complain when it comes to an end for us or for a loved one; rather, we may look back in satisfaction when it has been bravely and honorably withstood.

Albert Einstein, 1919
Collected Papers of Albert Einstein,
the Einstein Archives

Look deep, deep into nature, and then you will understand everything better.

Albert Einstein
after the death of his sister, Maja, in 1951
The New Quotable Einstein

This university is today a living thing, a home of free learning and teaching and happy collegial work. There it is, on the soil that our people have liberated under great hardships; there it is, a spiritual center of a flourishing and buoyant community whose accomplishments have finally met with the universal recognition they deserve.

Albert Einstein, 1949
in an address to the Hebrew University of Jerusalem

Israel is the only place on earth where Jews have the possibility to shape public life according to their own traditional ideals.

Albert Einstein, 1954
from an address to the American Friends of the
Hebrew University, in Princeton, New Jersey

Researchers hopeful to learn more about the genius of Einstein can find a wealth of information at their fingertips in a private home on a quiet street in Pasadena, California. In collaboration between the Hebrew University in Jerusalem and Caltech University in California, all of Albert Einstein's collected works are together under one roof for the sole purpose of further studying the mind and theories of this great man.

Called "The Einstein Papers Project," this enormous collection fills cabinets and file drawers on the entire first floor of the house. Some 65,000 documents—from scientific papers and Zionist and political statements, to intimate letters and scribbled notes from schoolchildren— have all been carefully preserved.

On the second floor of the house, where Dr. Diana Kormos Buchwald, the director of the project, can be found, are the volumes of *The Collected Papers of Albert Einstein*. This 30-volume series compiled of copies of the papers (the originals are kept in a bomb shelter at Hebrew University) has also been converted into electronic files, which are slowly becoming available to the public for purchase or for review at Einstein Archives Online (www. alberteinstein.info).

The Einstein Papers Project began in 1981 at Princeton University, then moved to Boston University, and then to the California Institute of Technology in 2000, when Dr. Buchwald (an associate professor) was named the new director. Since then, Dr. Buchwald and her team of researchers have been hard at work completing the 30-volume set at the rate of one volume every two years. They expect this incredible undertaking will take 40 more years to complete! Until then, anyone can surf the database of material at the Einstein Archives Online, or by visiting www.einstein.caltech.edu.

EINSTEIN'S BRAIN

We should take care not to make intellect our god; it has, of course, powerful muscles, but no personality.

Albert Einstein, 1943
Out of My Later Year

When Albert Einstein died, researchers thought that by studying his brain they might find a clue to his genius. So before he was cremated, a pathologist named Thomas Harvey removed his brain. It was supposed to have been kept secret, but word eventually spread that the great physicist's brain had been removed. The story then made headlines around the world.

What happened to the brain?

Albert Einstein's brain has had a pretty remarkable journey since his death in 1955. For many years, Dr. Harvey kept the brain preserved in two glass mason jars at his home in Wichita, Kansas, in a cardboard box in his basement. Dr. Harvey marked the box, "Costa Cider."

Most of the brain, except for the cerebellum and parts of the cerebral cortex, had been cut into 240 pieces.

Over the years, Dr. Harvey gave pieces of Einstein's brain to different researchers. When he and his wife separated, Dr. Harvey took the remainder of the brain from the basement when he moved out. He traveled around the country after that, taking the brain with him wherever he went! Dr. Harvey finally moved back to Princeton in 1996 and gave the remaining pieces of the brain to Dr. Elliot Krauss, the chief pathologist at Princeton Hospital.

What has been learned from Einstein's brain?

Researchers have weighed the brain, measured different parts of the brain and studied its composition, hopeful that they would get a clue as to why Albert Einstein was so smart. But they soon discovered that the size of a brain doesn't tell anything about a person's intelligence. One scientist at the University of California at Berkeley did report that he'd discovered an above-average number of "glial" cells in Einstein's brain's left hemisphere—an area associated with math and language skills.

Although it is intriguing to use the results of these researchers as an indication that Einstein's genius was related to a particular region of his brain, it's important to point out that when his brain was studied, it was compared to other brains in order to make conclusions. These other brains may not have been the best group for comparison, since the average age of those brains was twelve years younger than his.

So the question remains: What made Albert Einstein so smart?

Yes, his brain was different—but everyone's brain is unique. And perhaps the regions of his brain that had more glial cells made him better equipped to become a great mathematical thinker. But to find the truth, we cannot only look at the study of his brain, but we must also look into the life and times of Albert Einstein, the individual. His upbringing, his education, and the choices he made, the world he lived in—all had a major impact on his intelligence. Einstein's life was full of triumphs and tragedies. Indeed, his Jewish roots may have been a factor in his intelligence; and so might have been the genes he inherited from his parents and grandparents. Or perhaps it was his intense passion for music, art, math, and science that helped develop his intellectual mind.

Then again, Albert Einstein's genius may even have been sparked by that small compass he received from his father as a little boy.

Banesh Hoffmann, a close friend and an Einstein biographer, tells how when the two men were engrossed in a discussion about problem they could not solve, Albert would often pace the floor, twirl a lock of his long, white hair around his finger and say, in broken, accented English: "I vill a little t'ink."

PEOPLE OF NOTE
IN ALBERT EINSTEIN'S LIFE

Michele Angelo Besso A close friend of Einstein's during his years at the Zurich Polytechnic Academy and then at the patent office in Bern, Switzerland. Besso was a mechanical engineer who shared Einstein's affinity for classical music.

Helen Dukas A Swabian woman whom Einstein hired as his personal secretary in 1928. Helen traveled with the Einsteins on lecture tours, moved with them to the United States in 1933, and cared for Einstein after the death of Elsa in 1936.

Hermann Einstein Einstein's father, a merchant and engineer.

Pauline Einstein Einstein's mother, a talented musician.

Maria (Maja) Einstein Einstein's younger sister.

Marcel Grossman Einstein's friend and fellow student at the Zurich Polytechnic Academy. Einstein, who often skipped his classes, relied upon Grossman's lecture notes to pass exams. Grossman's father helped Einstein secure a job at the Swiss Patent Office.

Elsa Lowenthal Einstein's cousin who became his second wife (after Mileva Maric). Elsa came to Germany to nurse Einstein back to health during a prolonged sickness. Einstein moved in with Elsa in 1917 and they were married in 1919. He adopted Elsa's daughters, Ilse and Margot, and they moved with Einstein to America in 1933. Elsa lived with him at Princeton University until her death in 1936.

Mileva Maric   Einstein's fellow student at the Zurich Polytechnic Academy and later his first wife. A Serbian woman who walked with a limp, she belonged to the Greek Orthodox Church and was of lower social standing than the Einstein family. Einstein's parents opposed the marriage but his father eventually give Albert his blessing. When Einstein moved to Berlin in 1914, the couple separated and Mileva and their sons returned to live in Zurich, Switzerland.

Max Talmud   A young, Jewish medical student who ate Thursday night dinners with the Einstein family when Albert was a child in Munich. Talmud introduced Einstein to books about philosophers and scientists. He shared his ideas and books with Albert.

Chaim Weizmann   Born in Motol, Russia in 1874, in the early 1900s he became active in the Zionist movement, and in 1905 he was elected to the General Zionist Council. In 1918 he was appointed head of the Zionist Commission and sent to Palestine by the British government to advise them on the future development of the country. With Einstein's fund-raising help, he was able to secure the money to build the Hebrew University in Jerusalem. Chaim Weizmann was chosen to serve as the first President of Israel, a role he filled until his death in 1952.

A TIMELINE OF
ALBERT EINSTEIN'S LIFE

1879   Albert Einstein is born in Ulm, Germany.

1880   Einstein family moves to Munich.

1881   Albert's sister Maja is born.

1884   Young Albert sees a compass for the first time, which makes a great impression on him.

1885   Albert enters the Petersschule, a Catholic primary school.

1888   Albert enters the Luitpold Gymnasium in Munich.

1894   Albert's family moves to Milan, Italy, but Albert stays in Munich to finish school. He quits school at the end of the year and joins his family in Italy.

1895   Albert moves to Aarau, Switzerland, hoping to enter the Federal Polytechnical Institute in Zurich. At age 16, writes his first scientific essay, "On the Investigation of the State of Ether in a Magnetic Field."

1896   In the fall, Albert graduates from the Aarau school in Switzerland, enabling him to enter the Federal Polytechnical Institute in Zurich.

1897   Albert meets Michele Besso, "the best sounding board in Europe."

1899   Albert meets Mileva Maric, whom he will later marry.

1900   Albert graduates from the Polytechnical Institute.

1901   Albert becomes a Swiss citizen.

1902   Albert starts work at the Swiss Patent Office in Bern. He and Mileva have a daughter, Lieserl, who is believed to have tragically died a year later from scarlet fever.

1902   Albert's father, Hermann, dies.

1903   Albert marries Mileva Maric.

1904   Albert's son Hans Albert is born.

1905   Albert completes writing of seminal papers during his "annus mirabilis."

1906   Albert is promoted to technical expert, second class, at the patent office.

1907   Albert has the "happiest thought of my life"—that gravity and acceleration are the same—allowing him to develop the theory of general relativity.

1908   Albert becomes a lecturer at the University of Bern in Switzerland.

1909   Albert is appointed extraordinary professor of Theoretical Physics at the University of Zurich.

1910   Albert's son Eduard is born.

1911   Albert is appointed director of the Institute of Theoretical Physics at the German University of Prague.

1912   Albert resigns from the German University and accepts appointment as professor of Theoretical Physics at the Swiss Federal Institute of Technology in Zurich.

1914   Albert accepts an appointment as professor at University of Berlin and moves to Germany.

1914   War breaks out and Mileva returns to Zurich with their sons.

1916   Albert publishes the "The Origins of the General Theory of Relativity." He becomes president of the German Physical Society.

1917   Albert becomes ill and is confined to bed for nearly nine months. In October, he begins directorship of the Kaiser Wilhelm Institute of Physics.

1919   Albert divorces Mileva and marries Elsa Lowenthal.

1919   Solar eclipse evidence confirms Einstein's predictions in his general theory of relativity. Later in the year, Albert becomes interested in Zionism.

1920   Albert's mother, Pauline, dies.

1921   Abert goes on world tour to support Zionism. He makes first trip to the United States with Chaim Weizmann on a fund-raising tour on behalf of the Hebrew University of Jerusalem.

1921   Albert receives the Nobel Prize in physics.

1923   Albert makes first trip to Palestine.

1928   Albert collapses and is again confined to bed. He hires Helen Dukas as his secretary and housekeeper.

1930   Albert learns son, Eduard, is mentally ill. First grandchild, Bernhard, is born to Hans Albert and his wife, Frieda.

1933   Albert leaves Germany for the United States and accepts a position at Institute of Advanced Study in Princeton, NJ. He publishes excerpts from his 1932 letters to and from Sigmund Frued entitled *Why War?*

1934   Albert's stepdaughter Ilse dies at age 37, after a long illness.

1935   Albert moves to 112 Mercer Street in Princeton, New Jersey, with Elsa, Margot, Maja, and Helen Dukas.

1936   Albert's wife Elsa dies of heart and kidney disease.

1939   Albert writes famous letter to President Roosevelt to encourage the research of nuclear weapons.

1939   World War II begins in Europe.

1940   Albert becomes an American citizen (but still retains his Swiss citizenship).

1941   United States enters World War II.

1945   World War II ends.

1946   Albert becomes chairman of the Emergency Committee of Atomic Scientists. He urges the United Nations to form a world government to maintain world peace.

1948   Albert's wife, Mileva dies in Zurich.

1948   Albert learns he has an abdominal aneurysm.

1951   Albert's sister, Maja, dies in Princeton.

1952   Albert declines an offer to become the second President of Israel.

1955   Albert Einstein dies in Princeton as a result of a ruptured aorta.

1965   Albert's son Eduard dies.

1973   Albert's son Hans Albert dies.

1982   Helen Dukas dies.

1986   Albert's stepdaughter Margot dies.

1987   Volume 1 of *The Collected Papers of Albert Einstein* is published. (Nine Volumes have been published as of 2005.)

2005   The 100th Anniversary of Einstein's "annus mirabilis" is celebrated around the world.

REFERENCES

Books

Beckjard, Arthur. *Albert Einsten*. New York: G.P. Putnam's Sons, 1959.

Brian, Denis. *Einstein: A Life*. New York: John Wiley & Sons, Inc., 1996.

Calaprice, Alice. *The New Quotable Einstein*. Princeton, New Jersey: Princeton University Press, 2005.

———. *Dear Professor Einstein*. New York: MJF Books, 2002.

Clark, Ronald W. *Einstein: The Life and Times*. New York: The World Publishing Company, 1971.

Cwiklik, Robert. *Albert Einstein and the Theory of Relativity*. Hauppauge: Barron's Educational Series, 1987.

Dank, Milton. *Albert Einstein*. New York: Franklin Watts, 1983.

Forsee, Aylesa. *Albert Einstein: Theoretical Physicist*. New York: The Macmillan Company, 1963.

Goldenstern, Joyce. *Albert Einstein: Physicist and Genius*. Berkeley, New Jersey: Enslow Publishers, Inc., 1995.

Sammartino McPherson, Stephanie. *Albert Einstein*. Minneapolis: Lerner Publications Company, 2003.

Wise, William. *Albert Einstein: Citizen of the World*. Farrar, Straus & Cudahy Inc.; Philadelphia: Jewish Publication Society, 1960.

Published Papers

Beck, Anna, and Peter Havas. *The Collected Papers of Albert Einstein, Volume 1, The Early Years: 1879–1902*. Princeton, New Jersey and Oxford: Princeton University Press and Hebrew University of Jerusalem, 1987.

Winteler-Einstein, Maja. *Albert Einstein—A Biographical Sketch*. Princeton: Princeton University Press; Jerusalem: Hebrew University of Jerusalem, 1987.

Periodicals

The International Jerusalem Post, Jerusalem, March 26, 2004.

Scientific American, September, New York, 2004.

Web Sites

http://www.alberteinstein.info Einstein Archives Online.

http://www.einstein.caltech.edu The Einstein Papers Project.

http://www.pbs.org/wgbh/nova/einstein/genius/index.html.

http://nobelprize.org/physics/laureates/1921/einstein-bio.html.

http://www.aip.org/history/einstein The Center for History of Physics, American Institute of Physics.

http://www.albert-einstein.org, Albert Einstein Archives.

http://faculty.washington.edu/chudler/neurok.html. Neuroscience for Kids.

http://www.princetonhistory.org/einstein.cfm.

http://www.jewishmag.com/59mag/einstein/einstein.htm.

INDEX